Clare Cameron

A HUMAN AND SPIRITUAL JOURNEY

Clare Cameron in the thirties

Clare Cameron

A
Human
and Spiritual
Journey

BRIAN GRAHAM

LONDON:
WERNER SHAW LTD.
1984

TO CLARE

You will always occupy a
special place in my heart.

© BRIAN GRAHAM, 1984

ISBN 0 907961 03 7

Printed and bound in Great Britain for
the publishers, Werner Shaw Limited,
26 Charing Cross Road (Suite 34), London
WC2H 0DH. Typeset in 11 on 13 pt. Janson
with quotations in 10 on 11½ pt. Janson
by Alacrity Phototypesetters, Banwell Castle,
Weston-super-Mare. Jacket design by Alan Downs

Contents

Acknowledgements

I am deeply grateful to all who have helped make this book possible: those who kindly sent me their recollections of Clare; Sheilah Reeve for sorting and filing eighty-six years of material and for re-typing part of the manuscript; Enid Edgeley and Betty Martin for re-typing the remainder. I would also like to thank my mother and father who attended to the practical running of my home and much else while I was involved in the book; those friends who encouraged and supported me in my task, particularly Patty Bundy; and Barry Shaw who gave me the opportunity and believed I could do it. To everyone named and un-named I extend my heartfelt appreciation.

Preface

On the morning of 9 March 1983 I sat by the hospital bedside of Clare Cameron as she lay dying, her hand clasped in mine. She was partly unconscious, her small body so still upon the bed. Though she could not speak I felt she knew I was there. I thought of the anxious daily visits over the last five weeks and how much her condition had deteriorated in the past few days. I heard myself silently repeating, 'Fly away little one to that Golden Shore'. Over and over I silently sung those words. I looked at my watch — it was 8.55 a.m. I looked at Clare's face, the troubled lines above the closed eyelids. Then, quite suddenly, her hand squeezed mine and her body went into a contraction as if she was about to give birth. In that moment of labour her body gave birth to her soul which took flight to that Golden Shore beyond the door of death. I did not experience her death but an incredible moving experience of birth. I stood up, kissed her brow and noticed how peaceful and beautiful her body looked. Before me I did not see the body of an old lady but that of an old and wise-looking Tibetan man.

Clare was a special soul, friend and companion who, in the fourteen years that I had the privilege to know her, gave me, through the closeness of our friendship, more than words can ever say.

She was very much an individual and mystic in her own right, one who was blessed with a vision of the unity of all things in God. Her wisdom, her deep belief in God, her perception of truth and beauty inspired and confirmed the awakening which has taken place in myself and in many others over the years.

She often referred to herself as a universalist for she was very much aware of the divine ground which all men and women walk upon and she embraced with her heart and understanding all of mankind and the many sincere and different ways to God.

She was, amongst many things, a bridge between the younger

generation and the older, and a bridge between the world of men and the world of angels. She was also very much a human being, with struggles, fears and limitations but, most of all, she had a loving and accepting nature. She knew the pain of individual transformation and, because of her own experiences of such struggles, she knew what others went through; she has been a great help to many over the years.

She believed that life does not end with the dying of the physical body and I know that her soul walks now in beauty on a distant shore.

She was loved and thought very finely of by many and though she is no longer physically with us, her presence will always occupy a very special place in my heart and in the hearts of many others all over the world.

I wish for you, dear Clare ... peace and fulfilment as you walk that distant shore, hand in hand with God. May the spirit of truth, beauty and love which you instilled in us all, forever sustain you.

Through her writings, her poetry and the special person that she was, she had a rare and very valuable ability to touch deeply the innermost recesses of the soul, helping spiritually to awaken numerous travellers on their journey and search for greater meaning and purpose in life. She always said that she could completely accept the fears and failings in others because she had so many in herself.

Another very close friend of Clare's spoke of her '.... being of the warrior caste — without a doubt — she had the ability to go on battling through to the very end making so much possible that would otherwise only have been in the realm of dreams'.

DOWN BY THE QUAY

I remember the night
We went down to the quay
And gazed in silent wonder
At the stars on the sea.

And smiling we shared
The birth from night's womb
Of three pure white swans
Wings lit by the moon.

I have many fond memories

That will always remain
And down by the quay, Clare,
I shall meet you again.

In the following pages of her biography I have attempted to portray the human and spiritual parts of her nature in the hope that, by revealing the special person that she was, others too may awaken to a deeper perception of beauty and the true meaning of life.

UNIVERSAL

I am green earth's daughter,
Sister to the wind and water
And fathered by the sun.
From an ancient magic
Fashioned was my fabric
Ere the flesh was spun.

Where the deer are running
Habitation shunning,
Swiftly through the glade,
With all shy and wild things
On powerful or bright wings
There my track is made.

White snow of December
And the glowing ember
Of the autumnal tree,
Stillness of the moonlight
And the grace of moth-flight
Also dwell in me.

Where the birds are questing
Find my spirit resting
In trackless path of sky,
The privileged partaker
Of Being, and my Maker,
In His breast to lie.

O beautiful, my kindred,
Come ye then unhindered,
Passing through, yet free.
For there is no telling
The boundary of my dwelling
To far infinity.

I am green earth's daughter,
Sister to wind and water
And fathered by the sun,
To share with you the essence
Of the Eternal Presence
And quicken everyone ...

                                              C.C.

1

Early Days — Human and Spiritual

On 10 May 1896 a seed was planted in the form of a sensitive and artistic soul in the deprived soil of London's East End. Little was it known at the time that this gifted soul was to grow into a fine rare flower whose essence, through the medium of her beautiful poetry, inspired writings and the unique person that she was, would touch the depths of the hearts of many thousands of people all over the world. She was blessed with a deep understanding of the human and divine nature of man and of the beauty of nature in its many forms.

Christened Winifred Clara Wells (she later adopted the pseudonym of Clare Cameron) her early days were spent in a very different London to that which we know today. Her father, to whom she felt close, was a blacksmith by trade and her mother, whom Clare always felt was too strict, had at one time been a court dresser. They were an honest, caring, hard-working couple, struggling to provide the daily bread and maintain a secure homelife. They lived in a small terraced house at 140 Plashet Lane, East Ham in a gloomy grey environment where the stunted branches of the trees aspired in vain to touch the blue beyond the city clouds.

Born with a craving for beauty in nature, art and literature she was quite different from her companions and sought to escape from her sordid surroundings. She longed for the woods, the open country, natural wilderness to which she fled when rare opportunity offered. Those days of escaping from the confines of the city were few and far between, to be 'collected like beads on a string.' More often she spent a Saturday evening at a music-hall, where grown-ups laughed unaccountably at clumsy tramps with red noses and applauded fat ladies in pink who sang, or she visited the big market with its strange smells and noises with women pushing and pulling for bargains — exciting but bewildering to a sensitive little girl.

1

Clare described her everyday life in this way:

> Day was ugly and hard. Day for everybody meant work and a constant battle with the distasteful — with sweeping and cleaning and washing and looking after babies, in a coarse apron with sleeves rolled up till after tea-time for almost everybody. Day meant serviceable, ugly clothes, stiff serges and heavy boots, hard words and few smiles and bullying little boys who shouted horrid and shameful things, as they chased a frightened little girl and ran away laughing.*

One of her first mystical experiences occurred when she was a young girl wiping dry the dishes as her mother washed them:

> The hammer rang on the leather and the dishes rattled in the enamel bowl. A shaft of sunlight darted through the muslin curtain of the small window and lit the whitewashed wall, and above the curtain there was clear blue sky. Tim sat on a chair by the sink and watched us. Then something happened. Suddenly I was no more aware of the ringing of the hammer or the watching cat. And yet they were there, intensified and sharpened into clearer outline by a light that was not of the everyday. Light, light ... as sudden as lightening ... out of nowhere ... It was all around me in great tumbling waves of joy and peace and beautiful serenity. Life stood still, crystallized. The moment was a jewel, flawless, perfect, and shining with a radiance I have never before known. Life was calm and strong and beautiful and glorious beyond words, and it was all true. I *knew* it was true. I could see it, here in the light. I stood on a peak. I was God, and about my head beat all the music of the spheres ... Tim jumped from his chair with a thud, and there was father bending over mother's worn shoe just the same, and here was I wiping dishes and hanging cups upon their hooks. The moment had passed. The light was out. Life was thick and grey again, without colour, without a song, without joy, without peace. It tasted like wool; it was heavy, slow and cold. There was only the evening sunlight through the window. It had been funny, that. But I would never, never forget.

Clare never did forget this early experience and on a number of occasions over the years she recollected very vividly this expansion of perception. She was born into this life with ancient memories of a higher state of consciousness and bore the imprint it had on her in the mystic, hazy quality that emanated from her eyes.

---

* This and subsequent quotations in Chapter One, except where otherwise stated, are from Clare Cameron's autobiography, *Rustle of Spring*, first published in 1927 by Cecil Palmer; reprinted 1979 by Skilton & Shaw.

Clare with
her father

Below: With
teacher and
class-mates.
Clare is third
from the left
in back row

She was ambitious, eager to learn, always reaching out for something better, with that deep awareness of beauty which gives as much pain as joy; hungry for books, for music, for the kind of friendship where there is a mutual understanding of the aspirations and longings of the soul. Her love of writing developed into a love of making verses. Her family were affectionate towards her but misunderstood her yearning and oppressed her intelligence, offering her little criticism of the right kind.

Just before Clare's teenage years, her brother Cliff was born and some of her time was spent taking her young brother around the neighbourhood streets in a push-chair.

Clare often recollected how excited she was when, in 1909, aged thirteen, her first short story was printed in the *Young Citizen*, following a literary competition:

> My story was printed, and there was my name and school in full above it! And I might choose for a prize two tins of Mackintosh's toffee, *or* a pocket knife, *or* a piece of art needlework for embroidery. I did not think about that, for my pulses were racing and my head buzzing with the glorious words: 'I am in print! I am in print!' My feet were feathers as I raced through the dark streets, the precious paper clasped in my arms, and seeing nothing but the golden avenues of the future shining before me. My impetuosity almost knocked mother over as she opened the door.
>
> '*Now* what is it?' She was a little irritable, but stopped to wipe her hands on her apron as I pointed with triumphant finger to the emblazoned page. Her indifference slowly thawed to incredulous wonder: 'Well, I never, then! What will you choose? I should have the art needlework ...'
>
> Quite late, up in my room, calm and reasonable again, I sank on my knees before the window under the starlit sky and felt rather small and weak, and very grave, as though a tremendous mission were laid upon me. There seemed nothing funny about it. Life was very serious.
>
> The clouds passed over the stars, high, remote, inscrutable. The future was veiled like the sky, but to me full of promise and unrevealed glory.

This first short story portrayed Clare's compassion and perception into the caring nature of man, often hidden by the shell of indifference and selfishness:

REVENGE!

It was evening on Burnley Marshes, and the shadows were lengthening as the sun slowly set and the day began to fade. Harry Melton, a tall boy of fourteen summers, and dressed in a scout's suit, and his pole in his hand, picked his way carefully over the boggy land, which held no dangers for him, having lived there all his life. He belonged to the 1st Antrim Troop of Scouts, and was one of the best and most enterprising boys of his troop. With a happy heart he stepped lightly over the grassy but deceiving land, homeward. Suddenly he stopped. What was that cry? Faint, but surely a cry for help! It was dark, and what terrors might that marsh hold? But, above all, a precious human life was in peril, some helpless one might be in danger, sinking, sinking into the dark, thick mud, down to a terrible death! But, stifling his terrors, he tightened his hold on his staff, and set out towards the way, dangerous though it was, from whence the sound came. Hark! there it was again, but fainter. Was the victim even now dying in indescribable agony?

Soon he reached the spot and looked about him. There was what he had come to save! Not a tiny child, or a baby; not an unwary stranger, but Harry's great enemy — a great, cowardly bully, who only the day before thrashed two little urchins, after tying Harry to a tree after a great struggle.

And now! What a chance for revenge! Did a dishonourable and thoroughly wicked bully deserve to be rescued? But Harry had no time for meditation, no time for muse; nor had the bully any time to repent of his wicked deeds to Harry and others. A great struggle went on in the scout's mind; should he yield to temptation? No, he must save him. It was not for one of England's boys to shirk his duty, in danger or in peace.

With one bound he was at the sinking boy's side and, though in great peril of sinking himself, put forth his whole strength and gradually, ah! how slowly! pulled him out of the bog.

'Saved!' murmured the rescued boy, 'And — by you? To whom I've been so wicked!'

'Let us forget the past!' said Harry, 'and go home rejoicing in the present.'

Stronger and stronger grew the desire in Clare to pursue a literary career. Evidence of her ability was present from this early age and was remarked on by her head teacher when she was almost four-teen. At that time, April 1910, she was attending Hartlet Avenue Girl's School and remarks on her report read:

Her work in the Ex-V11 Standard has been marked by a desire to do her best at all times, by careful thought and refinement of mind. She has shown considerable imaginative power in the way she has treated the various subjects set for composition. A subject in which she shows more than ordinary ability.

Furthermore, while attending East Ham Higher Elementary School, in her report for the term ending midsummer 1911, she achieved the top position in her class, gaining 240 marks for English out of a maximum of 250 marks; a special comment was added at the end of this report; 'Special mention must be made of the more than average ability shown in English.'

Clare, in later years, attributed her success in English and composition at school to a teacher who recognized her writing ability and did all she could to encourage and support her in this field.

Beauty and truth strongly beckoned her and, discontented with the East London life, she sought solace in the works of Ruskin, Emerson, Lamb, Hazlitt, Whitman, Richard Jefferies, Coleridge, Tennyson, and Shelley as well as the modern poets. A prolonged course of romantic and inspiring reading further intensified her desire to seek a different way of life; her determination to break through the web of circumstance began to grow stronger.

Early in her adolescent years she met a young man called Paul who had a 'quiet voice and gentle caressive hands'. In Paul she found a kindred spirit, hungry, wanting things, discovering things, loving things, just like her. They enjoyed many tender youthful moments together.

Her need for self-expression prompted her to write:

> When I hear soft music, when I read grand lines of the grand poets, when I dream of wild scenes and wonderful places — oh, how it all hurts over me — and I can't tell it. What is it all saying — the lovely green earth and the wide blue sky, people and things and places. I know what it is saying, but I can't tell anybody! I want to! I want to! Dear God, let me out of myself, give me a voice! The first lines of a poem came into my head:
>
> > "O make a reed of music out of me,
> >   O thou most High,
> > That I may voice each melody
> >   Of earth and sky!"

There was so much more in Clare that she wanted to discover, to draw out and she remembered one evening when, just before going to bed, she stepped out into the garden:

> There was a fresh wind blowing. Out in the garden it was all dark beneath and bright above. Stars were tangled in the elderberry-tree a pitiful, stunted thing by day, with no colour in its leaves, leaning over the black fence disconsolately, but a living thing for me by night. My

face against its rough bark, I would talk to it in the dark, and pretend I heard its answer in the wind that played through its branches. We talked like friends. I told it personal, intimate things that sounded silly to other people. 'Tree, little tree, I love you. You know all of me that I can't explain to anyone else. Not even Paul. Things that make me want to cry because they're so beautiful ... Little tree, I believe you're very wise! Somehow you seem to teach me, to help me. Help me now. I am so hungry, and I don't know what I want! All these stars and this great space of sky .... I want to hug it all in my arms. I want ... What do I want? Comfort me! You're so firm and strong. I love you for your quietness. I can rest in you, darling little tree.'

There was a light in my room. Mother had lit my candle and was pulling down the blind. I kissed the tree in the dark, and went in, and upstairs to bed.

Of all God's handiwork, Clare had a very special love of trees and often she would sit beside one and commune with it, or lie on the grass looking up through the branches or give one a hug. She continued and cherished this special relationship with trees right up until her death.

In this early period of Clare's life she much looked forward to the family's annual holiday at Clacton; and just before departing on one of these trips she wrote:

Tomorrow to the sea, and the poppies in the corn and white ships a sailing! Then began beautiful times of lonely wanderings. When the ugly East End suburb was forgotten in the sunny freedom of long, unclouded days. Every day I sauntered along to the lonely cornfields on the cliffs, and lay on my back in the fierce sunshine, with larks climbing above and the whisper of the sea below, or wandering slowly along by the sea's edge to sandy solitudes beyond the crowd, thinking nothing and desiring nothing, but feeling the sun and the wind and the clean, bright air entering into me at every pore. I was no longer a restless child with locked lips and furrowed brow, but a collection of senses basking in elemental joys. It was glorious to stand at the edge of the cliff high above the sea and with outflung arms to greet the world. Maurice Hewlett had said somewhere: "I got up the mountain edge, and from the top saw the world stretch out — cornlands and forest, the river winding among meadow flats, and right off, like a hem of the sky, the moving sea, with snatches of foam, and large ships reaching forward, outbound. And then I thought no more, but my heart leapt to meet the wind, and I ran and ran. I felt my legs under me, I felt the wind buffet me, hit me on the cheek; the sun shone, the bees swept past me singing; and I too sang, shouted, World, World, I am coming!"

Oh, how I felt like that too! I didn't want even Paul out there, not anybody. Nature was sufficient for every need. She fed, satisfied, stimulated, sustained.

Time was passing too quickly. Back in the everyday life of East London her heart was restless again. There were vast realms of knowledge to be explored. At school she read Kipling and Belloc for the first time as they sang of Sussex and the green roads of England; her heart danced with joy at the lines of Belloc:

> I never get between the pines
> But I smell the Sussex air,
> Nor I never come on a belt of sand
> But the old place is there . . . .

She devoured the short stories of Kipling and blessed the local library which, for a penny a year, fed her with Tennyson, Keats, Shelley, Byron, William Morris, the Sonnets of Shakespeare, and the Rossettis and the lyrics of the Elizabethan writers. It was with such inspired men that she found sanctuary, a garden wherein she could breathe the scent of precious flowers:

> The day was fast approaching when I must leave school, for I was nearly fifteen and must do my small share to support the family income. I was sorry, for it meant the loss of my freedom and the sudden stoppage of that inflow of knowledge that for the last few years I had recognized to be so precious. It did not occur to me that I might find greater wisdom in the world than any to be found in books. Then I should see less of Paul. No more should I discover his small figure with the rest of the girls at four o'clock, nor meet his gentle, welcoming smile as we fell into step together on the homeward way.

Clare's mother wished to apprentice her to dressmaking since she herself knew the trade, but it was the dream of Clare's heart to get amongst books somehow, somewhere. It was at this time that the thought occurred to her to seek employment in a newspaper office. One of the first letters which she wrote was to a Mr Cadbury of the *Daily News*; it read:

> Dear Sir,
> I am writing to you for help and advice.
>   Having an ability in writing, I have a great and long-cherished desire to follow a literary career. But having no literary friends at all to help me, I find myself in difficulty. I have been advised to write very little during the next three or four years, but to study well the works of the

best authors and cultivate their styles; but not being in a position to do this, and hearing of you as a well-known, kindly gentleman, I am writing to you for help.

I am fifteen years of age, and have contributed short stories to children's magazines; also I have good testimonials from my former school-mistress.

I am aware that I must start at the foot of the journalistic ladder, but I have no one to help me to get a footing. Is it, therefore, in your power to help me?

I cannot place my MSS. for publication without the payment of large fees which, my Father being merely an artisan, I can ill afford. Also, it is necessary that I should quickly earn money.

Most fervently hoping that you will be able to help so young and struggling an authoress.

>				I am,
>			Yours truly
>			Miss Winifred Wells

It was to this request that she received the following reply on 9 October 1911:

Dear Madam,

Mr Henry T. Cadbury asks me to let you know that, while he cannot make you any definite promise of assistance, he would like to see you with reference to your letter to him of the 5th.

Perhaps you could arrange to call at these offices at 12 noon tomorrow, Tuesday. If you cannot manage this, Mr Cadbury could meet you at the same time on Wednesday. When you arrive, please ask for the undersigned.

>			Yours truly,
>			T. G. Curtis

Clare did manage to keep this first appointment and, in a letter dated 10 October 1911, she received the following:

Dear Madam,

Further to our conversation this morning, I am prepared to offer you a position here at 7/6 a week to start with, the hours being from 2 to 7 p.m. except on Saturdays, when they will be different and shorter. As these hours by no means constitute a full day's work, we should expect you at the same time to be taking lessons in shorthand and typewriting.

I should be glad if you could take up your duties here on Monday next at 3 p.m. Please enquire for Miss Fletcher on your arrival.

>			Yours truly,
>			Per Pro The Daily News, Limited
>			H. T. Cadbury — Managing Director

And so began the first step of Clare's literary career in the offices of the *Daily News* in Bouverie Street, London. Her duties involved the filing of cuttings from daily journals and assisting generally in minor office tasks.

On her employer's advice she began in the mornings a course on shorthand and typing at a school in Barking Road; it wasn't long before she was taken on fulltime at her work and her wages doubled. Nevertheless, her soul felt lost and desolate in the stark, grey indifferent city:

> Grey veils of vapour hid the blue of the sky, and the faces of the children as they dashed home, shrieking and calling down the many side-streets on their way from school, showed neither intelligence nor innocence. There was no one at the school with whom I could be intimate, or to whom I could unburden my full heart. The beauty of London failed to touch me at this time. And I was so tired, day by day and night by night. Sleep and oblivion was the great blessing of the day to which I looked forward and which I was loath to break every morning. I wanted Paul no longer. I wanted nobody, nothing, but to find a place under the sky where the air was sweet and the grass long and soft for aching limbs.

Feeling very alone Clare immersed herself in poetry and romances and the works of famous writers whose lines and verses fed her hunger for beauty and truth:

> I wrote lots of verses: verses about trees, the moon, the sea, the rain, the wind; of that ever-present need to open a gate within that would never yield more than an inch to let my emotions escape in song. I invoked God and praised Him when things went well, and questioned Him when they went ill, and threw off fragments of song to a vague Beloved whom I should meet one day and find a perfect friend.

It was at this time that she discovered, on the back page of a literary paper, an advertisement of a literary agency, The Authors' Alliance, which criticized amateur work for a very small fee. Carefully typing the best of her verses she sent them to the advertised address and received a long and supportive reply from a Mr Hatherley Clarke:

> ... We must congratulate you very heartily upon the high promise which your verses now indicate, and we think you should certainly cultivate the very real gift for poetry which you seem to possess. ... We have read with pleasure. They exhibit notable strength. ... At the same time we feel sure you will understand that there are heights which you have not yet reached. ...

This reply meant so much to Clare. It was confirmation that she could write poetry; that her lines had received a degree of recognition; that the door was open to that path in her life which she longed, in the depths of her heart, to walk along.

Clare's gift of writing verse, her sensitivity and perception of beauty certainly indicated much future promise in these early poems:

TO BEAUTY

O had I all about my feet
The flowers of life that men desire;
O could my days run glad and fleet
And bright as Spring to never tire,
And were all knowledge mine, to beat
About my soul in flakes of fire.

And had I swallow wings to soar
What time the day is passing by
Beyond the sunset's golden door,
And watch along with God on high
The seas of twilight break and pour
In waves of peace across the sky —

Yet ever would my happiness
On mocking wings rise up and flee,
And nought on earth have power to bless
Until my bursting heart were free
To sing the joy and sweet distress
That Beauty passing wakes in me.

SONG

If I could make a little song
As lovely as the skylark's is
A simple music sweet and strong
But soft and fleeting as a kiss;

A little song to truly tell
All that I am and long to be,
The tender hopes and dreams that swell
And so distress the heart and me;

Then would I come with quiet feet
My song made perfect in my hand,

> And nought on earth were then more sweet
> Than you should hear and understand.
>
> Alas! 'tis crying for the moon
> And sun and stars, that I would be!
> For I were God's archangel soon
> If I could sing such mystery.

Soon, the winds of change came and she lost her first job ... owing to a reduction of staff her employers were compelled to dispense with her services:

> I was out of work. I slipped back into the grey days of childhood so lately left behind, and missed the little money I had. There was nothing to give to Mother at the end of the week, and nothing to save for better clothes, and certainly none for books. The gates of beauty raised themselves high above me, inexpressibly lovely and desirable, but fast-barred and mocking and terribly remote. With head down I moved through the shadows of the lower air, and supposed something would turn up some time.

After many letters to various newspapers and magazines, something did turn up in the form of a position with a firm of law publishers, just off Fleet Street. A load was removed from Clare's mind. 'Now I could sleep again at nights, and wake without the shadow in the morning. It meant security again, a little money, a little freedom, change, a little progress in the struggle to the light.'

While at her new place of employment, a colleague expressed her admiration of Clare's poems. This inspired her to write more verses which gave escape to the needs of adolescence — she even began to see the elusive beauty and mystery of London.

The months passed, and her eighteenth birthday heralded a very memorable experience:

> It came in a little street off Charing Cross Road, one dusky evening, as I lingered among the books displayed in the boxes there. There was a shop I had entered two or three times, given courage by the sight of cheap volumes that were sometimes within reach of my purse.
>
> I had talked to the middle-aged bookseller there, shyly and awkwardly when I found him almost as shy as myself. The shop was empty, and he came from the back room with a smile of greeting. We agreed that late October dusks were more beautiful than any others, especially in this magical London. He brought out a new collection of

Whistler reproductions that he had obtained especially for a customer, and I thought them very beautiful.

'Come into the back room. There may be something there to interest you.' We were talking now of the satisfying things people found in life, of the scourge of materialism and the neglect of art, of the things that were so beautiful that they hurt, of the things that could give you the only real happiness — books, pictures, nature, philosophies, sciences, religions. We discussed the ancient religions of the world, and the new, and how they all met at the ultimate peak of truth. Then somehow, suddenly, we were talking no more; the voices ceased while the interchange of ideas went on unheard, invisible. Something had stopped. Life dropped away — or was it death that had dropped away leaving our souls burning with vitality upon a great peak in sunlight — in light that washed in great tranquil waves up and above and below and around, as it had swept round the feet of the child, wiping dishes in the scullery on a spring evening years ago? We were no longer two human beings fumbling with clumsy words to open the difficult doors of expression, no longer two minds that must be forever isolated, reaching out hungrily for contact, but one mind communing with itself, one soul filled with sublime content and mystic fiery peace that hungered for nothing and sought for nothing, for it possessed all.

My heart was shouting with exultation. This was the Truth, this was the Life, the Way, the only Joy, the only true Reality! This was the Light Eternal and I was among the spirits of God! But it was going — it was passing — like a door closing inevitably and swiftly.

If only life were always like this! This was the only thing that mattered. All things were made new, and I could see right through all the worlds. I prayed to the light about me; 'Teach my heart and my mind to understand what in this moment my soul knows! Stay — divine moment — stay till I know.' It was gone. The door was closed, the moment was past, in the winking of an eye. It could not be recaptured. This was real life after all. We were two people under a spluttering gas-jet staring silently and fixedly across a dusty room. The outlines were blurred; the thoughts moved slowly and thickly as they always did. One groped through the fog.

The voice of the man came awed and slow, almost a whisper, across the room: 'That was queer!'

I answered him as in a trance: 'I was God just now. I had all wisdom, all truth, all power. I was on a peak, and yet here all the time. Everything was sharpened and intensified a million times. Now it's all gone, in a flash.'

'I felt rather like that. What do you think it was?'

'The passing of the Holy Ghost, perhaps. Do you remember Pentecost, and the tongues of flame? It's happened to me before. When I was a little girl. Once or twice. I don't know how it comes, or why. It seems to happen to you anywhere, any time. You never know when the flash will come. You can't seek it and you can't hold it. It always seems to come unexpected, and for no reason. And it's always like that to me, catching you up out of life, crystallizing the moment, like frost on a pane.

'Life seemed to have stopped still. It was a revelation.'

'Perhaps it does, at those times. You can't say there's no God when you're privileged to feel like that, can you? You can't say there's no immortality of the soul .... Oh, words! ... I'm going. Good-night!'

It was dark in the court, and the stars spread serenely over in the strip of sky. I would remember. A tongue of flame. That moment — so beautiful and joyous and holy and altogether glorious. Oh, I must never be unhappy or hungry anymore, not really, for there was the Kingdom of Heaven — not a myth or a fable or a visionary's dream, but real.

Time went on, the seasons changed, the bookseller in the quiet court moved and Clare missed the precious times she had spent browsing through the treasures that lined the shelves which now stood barren and empty. Life seemed very grey again. She wanted so much to be loved and to pour out from her heart the gifts of herself upon the lover of whom she dreamed. Someone whom she could communicate with in mind and spirit. She became dissatisfied with her present employment and replied to an intriguing advertisement which she saw in the *Telegraph*; she was accepted on a month's trial in a publishing house, much grander than her previous places of employment. The future was again full of promise:

> Here the carpets were thick and soft to the feet, and the desks polished and roomy; there were books on the side, white mantlepieces and tasteful prints on the walls. I discovered that flowers looked well in such rooms; and the splash of colour in a selected corner delighted the eye. I gave the work great care, for I must do best to remain in this place where I knew more ease than I had ever known.

It was here that she became friends with a girl named Marjorie, who was her own age, a girl like herself who loved reading; who wanted to break away; an explorer; someone with whom she could share her feelings and opinions. Marjorie invited Clare to the grand opera at Covent Garden to see *Tristan and Isolde*. To Clare, grand opera was something traditional and artificial and didn't appeal to her; she felt it to be far removed from real life, but she consented to go and she was deeply affected by the performance, especially by the music of Wagner:

> Who was this Wagner with the voice of the sea on relentless shores, that was one and the same with the voice of the heart, swelling, falling, advancing, retreating, breath by breath, wave by wave? The voice of the blood, of surging water and leaping fire and fruitful earth, of hungry flesh and restless seeking soul, the voice of life — my voice. I flowed out to it and became one with the sea of sound, and in its mighty embrace was conscious of nothing but the ecstasy of union. Here I found something that had been mine since the beginning of time, long hidden, long held back.

That memorable night she realized that, within the stilted form of the opera, burned a radiant, living flame. The magnificent music of Wagner evoked and flooded the cavern of her heart and, stronger than ever, she felt that the composers of such powerful, soul-stirring music were indeed the most blessed of men. As Clare's life unfolded, such music had an ever-increasing and inspiring effect on her and on listening to the great composers she often felt in the company of angels.

Soon, the First World War was declared but life went on just the same and her thoughts very much lived in the future.

As the days unfolded in her new place of employment, Clare joyfully discovered that the young sub-editor, Mr Haliday, was also a poet and she gratefully appreciated studying the lines of this fellow dreamer and sharing her own verses with him. She also received a lot of support and praise from a senior colleague, Mr Vincent, for whom Clare had considerable respect. He assured her that her verses showed great promise.

> There were talks after office hours — great, inspiring, stimulating, disturbing, intoxicating talks, with Haliday the poet perched on a desk and his hands thrust deep in the pockets of his overcoat, the artist from downstairs drifting in for a moment of news, and Mr Vincent leaning up against the mantlepiece as with a swift ripple of speech and much play of thin hands he talked and talked. It seemed he understood all the distresses youth suffered, the perplexities and gropings in the dark, and brought his wisdom and his sense of humour to shine upon them and show them for what they were. Always there was much to ponder over, and many new threads to weave into one's thoughts.

These newly formed friendships with people who stimulated many of the fine thoughts and longings which Clare held, opened for her another door into a greater social life and "Bohemian"-orientated culture in which she felt very much at home. These new friends shared her love of music, beauty and the arts, of sweet and trembling passions.

When she was twenty-one, Clare set off on her first walking tour during a ten-day holiday period, her destination Sussex. Later in life, she was to return to the beautiful areas which she explored:

> The gipsy call of the white road. The clean and noble look of Petworth in the sunny morning; the Downs towering above Duncton and East Lavington in the stinging rain of a squally noon, the trees tossing in the wind and the pools rippling beneath her fingers, and the cheeks glowing with the chill, damp air ....
>
> Picturesque, tumbledown old cottages, whitewashed, and with bright curtains proclaiming the holiday-maker and the week-ender, dropped their worn steps to the shingly beach, and a houseboat sat solidly and silently round the bend of the harbour. It was high tide at Bosham, a village snug upon a backwater a few miles out of Chichester, and it was half-past twelve on a sunny June morning. It seemed a lonely, lost and quiet little place. Dawns would come gently over the placid water here, and sunsets sink their colours at the end of hot afternoons. There was no haste here, no burden, no frown, no struggle, only the ripple of the tide coming from the sea and returning in its appointed time. Gentle was the line of the shore, and careless and happy the leisurely fishermen and the barelegged children, the old cottages and the church in the trees.

Little did she know that, forty years later, she would return to Old Bosham and occupy one of these old cottages. This beautiful village held a special attraction for Clare to the very end of her life and to this day it is still known as peaceful Old Bosham and remains a favourite haunt for artists.

Back to London, bearing gifts for her family, her heart saturated with the beauty of the country, she felt renewed and glad to be alive and also happy with the warmth expressed by her family upon her return. Good news also awaited her — some of her verses had been accepted for publication in *Nash's Pall Mall Magazine*. Other poems had appeared in different periodicals around this time — life was becoming more meaningful and exciting:

IN MAY

One little shining hour
Fragrant and quiet and sweet,

At the end of a rain-swept day,
Pure as a dew-washen flower
You come and kneel at my feet,
Pure as a dew-washen flower
Little hour, stay!

A sweep of Time's silent wing,
Under the blossomed trees,
Over the sweet wet grass;
Love and the wonder of Spring,
Life, O scatter not these,
Love and the wonder of Spring,
As you pass! As you pass!

JOY — SONG

Happy, happy days, when the gods lean over
Their cloud-barred casements above, and throw
Blossoms of joy from the gardens of heaven
To the wistful hearts that hunger below!

Ah, slow-falling, the flowers are all about me,
One upon the hair for a shining crown of Youth,
One upon the eyes for the beauty of creation,
Twain upon the lips for the gifts of Love and Truth.

I will dance a path through the grey world and weary,
Flinging wide my flowers where no flowers will grow,
I will be your laughter, your courage and your comfort
Because I am young and the gods have blessed me so!

Soon came an invitation out to dinner by the artist from downstairs where Clare worked. This artist was actually a writer, Thomas Burke, who became quite a famous author in his day and was widely known for his books on Limehouse (the Chinese quarter of London), London inns and short stories. They began seeing each other, sharing their deepest thoughts, desires and dreams. Romance blossomed and on 9 September 1918, when Clare was twenty-two years old, they were married in East Ham Congregational Church, Wakefield Street, London.

In the same year, Clare's first poetry book, *The Three Crowns, and Other Poems*, was published and warmly praised by the critics. This first collection was dedicated to her husband and very much symbolized a breakthrough into new beginnings.

Clare Cameron

Thomas Burke

THE THREE CROWNS

Lord of Life, while youthful eyes
Shine with dreams of enterprise,
While Hope is strong to fight Despair
The laurel crown give us to wear.

But that our hearts may tuned be
To sweetness and simplicity,
Sometime place upon the head
A crown of thorn with berries red.

And ere we know that we are old,
And ere the fires of Love are cold,
Lord of Life, in tender wise
Strew the poppies in our eyes.

SEEKING

When the maiden morn arises
From her bed of purple gloom,
Wild desire my heart surprises —
Throbbing heart, for what, for whom?

All the day my soul unresting
Searches street and sky and face;
All the night my dreams are questing
In the starry fields of Space.

Ah, what is the wild, dear wonder,
Sweet Delight and Pain entwined,
Like a river running under
Hidden courtyards of the Mind?

To the great Heart-beat of Passion,
Through the stars our planet swings;
Every heart that Love doth fashion
Unto Love must lift its wings.

Therefore, Love, do I implore thee,
Draw the barring gates apart,
To the place thou madest for me
To an unknown human heart!

2

New Beginnings

Clare's marriage to Thomas Burke opened a door to a completely new life for her. His most famous book *Limehouse Nights*, a compilation of short stories, had just been published the previous year and had been praised by Arnold Bennett and H. G. Wells as of 'romantic force and beauty'. This compelling volume which brought him wide acclaim from many critics on both sides of the Atlantic also brought him lasting success and renown. Many other books flowed from his pen amongst which was *More Limehouse Nights*, especially dedicated to Clare. It was 'Tommy', as Clare affectionately called him, who introduced some of Clare's earlier work to London editors. This resulted in her writings becoming more widely known and in laying the firm foundations of her own literary success.

Clare's life was now much more exciting and meaningful; she met many writers, artists and playwrights, including several from across the Atlantic. One of the most famous of these was Charlie Chaplin who, at the height of his popularity, asked Tommy to take him round the Limehouse quarter of the East End of London, familiar to him as a boy. Clare often mused over this incident, recalling that, each time they stopped and were alighting from the taxi, a crowd quickly formed and voices cried out: 'There he is,' 'There he is,' 'There's Charlie!' and they had quickly to jump into the taxi and drive on. In his book *My Wonderful Visit*,* Charlie Chaplin writes of meeting Clare's husband and described Clare as: 'A very young lady of great charm, who makes you feel instantly her artistic capabilities even in ordinary conversation.'

In Tommy, Clare found a kindred spirit. Like herself he was sensitive, intuitive, artistic and loved good conversation. They both also shared a deep love of truth and were very much individualists.

*Published by Hurst & Blackett Ltd, London.

They saw through and denounced all humbug and cant and together were rare, outspoken figures in their day. They greatly complemented and encouraged each other in their individual literary careers.

When *The Three Crowns* was published, a reviewer in the *Aberdeen Journal* of 5 February 1919, spoke of Clare as "having a sensitive taste and never failing to sing agreeably". Another review which appeared in the *Southport Guardian* of 26 May 1920 described the writer as: 'A real singing bird, sensitively vibrant to every impression on youth yearning for love — yet recognising also the deeper, disciplinary virtues.'

Through her marriage Clare was much more in the public eye. On a visit to the Goupil Art Gallery, Regent Street she was mentioned in *The Westminster Gazette*, 6 January 1922: 'A dainty slim figure in grey, the wife of Mr Thomas Burke, the short-story writer, was among the early visitors to the private view of Hoppé portraits held yesterday.' The artist within her beckoned her to view many of the fine paintings that graced the walls of numerous London galleries and, being sensitive to the aspirations and forms of expression of other artists, she found inspiration and solace in her excursions.

As the wife of an acclaimed author and a poetess and writer of distinction herself, numerous articles of her own began to appear in the newspapers and periodicals of the day. One such article appeared on 30 May 1925 in *T.P.'s & Cassell's Weekly*:

WOMEN WHO KILL GENIUS
Limiting Power and Development

They are not always the scolds, the selfish bargainers who expect as much out of the contract of marriage as they are prepared to put into it, with interest; not always the masterful, unimaginative women whose lives are run within a hard and narrow circle to which all entering that circle must conform. Nor are they always slaves of convention, but often the sweet and tender women who are also slaves only to love, and whose only fault is the weakness of misunderstanding.

It is unfortunate that she, who was destined for man's companion and mate, should in various ways limit his powers and forbid him any development which is likely to take him from her side.

Yet through history there have been loving women who, consciously and unconsciously, have hindered and destroyed. One remembers how the wilful spirit of Harriet Westbrook fettered the winged spirit of Shelley, until it broke suddenly and irretrievably, hopelessly, and he found steadier and more lasting companionship in Mary Godwin. One thinks of the fretful Minna, the wife of Wagner — Minna of the nagging tongue and expensive tastes and quick temper — who for many years filled his creative life with wearying irritation and clung to him in tears each time he strove to leave her; of the scolding wife of Socrates, and the clinging unimaginative Anne whom Shakespeare married at eighteen; of the cold, intolerant Miss Milbanke whom the headstrong and passionate Byron chose for a wife; and of the vague unhappiness in the life of Dickens.

Since the world began the follies of men have made long and arduous reaping, have held their eyes to earth when they should be lifted to the stars, their songs fumbling in their throats for lack of spiritual freedom.

Should one not be sorry for them too — the trusting girls who find life with genius such a sorry business? Their road like Mary's road, dusty with hidden service as they tread it alone, giving up continually to the crowd that which they so long to retain for themselves — the full personality and expressive soul of the beloved?

Should genius marry at all? Perhaps not. But even your genius in noncreative moods is an ordinary man craving human contact and the quiet joys of the domestic hearth. One may also reply to such an indictment of the wives of genius with the assertion that too often has genius killed women, perhaps quite as often as women have killed genius.

The woman who marries genius must be prepared for much dis-illusion and sacrifice that the wife of the ordinary man never knows — she must tread the long road of forbearance and allow for failings of her mate as one excuses those of a child. For genius is a child, in his abstraction and nearness to spiritual realities; and she is mother, privi-leged above all other mothers, with her gifted but wayward nursling. Her love, however great and comprehensive, must never intrude or take liberties or make excessive demands, but remain steady and quiet in the background to help and inspire in silence and content. The hearth must be for him not a mechanism in which he plays the part of a well-oiled and obedient cog, but a place where there must be no rules.

And she must be patient — endlessly patient; maintaining always an attitude that in the humdrum relationships of ordinary people would be ridiculous in its meticulous fidelity. But none of this means self-abnegation. May she not foster interests of her own that shall assist her own development and happiness without retarding his, and yet remain faithful to her love for him? May she not be free, that he may be free? For to live happily with genius and allow it justice does not mean rebellion, resignation or submission. Here is not careless selfishness or slavish devotion, but a fearless recognition of facts and their intelligent adjustment to ordinary daily life. This is the real courage that not only steels the soul but engenders that common sense which is the highest wisdom, and without which progress through this imperfect world is clumsy and disastrous.

This fine article bore evidence of her own relationship with her husband who, in his own unique way, was a genius of his time; it also echoed her need to follow her own interests and partake of the quest for her spiritual development. Though their relationship nurtured a great degree of creativity through the written word in both Tommy and Clare, and fostered a mutual understanding and care for each other, there were also areas in which they had conflicting interests. Clare found it hard at times to be the endlessly patient wife always making sacrifices and striking a balance between this role and taking steps to assist her own development. Tommy was very much at home in London and he once said: 'As a born Londoner I cannot remember a time when London was not part of me, and I part of London.' Even though Clare had come to view London through different eyes than those through which she

viewed it when younger, her heart was very much drawn to the countryside; to the infinite expressions of Mother Nature and the meaning and beauty it instilled in the depths of her soul. Tommy's involvement with his writings was all-absorbing. Though Clare understood this strong need in him she later recalled, when talking about their relationship, that her own need for the love she had sought from one man wasn't being met. She felt restless, a restlessness which remained with her for the rest of her life, sometimes in the background, sometimes in front; a disturbing restlessness which she realized, towards the end of her life, caused her to pursue elusive butterflies which, when caught, would bring only temporary fulfilment. This restlessness brought its trials and tribulations, its pain and suffering but it also increased her deep longing to know God more fully and brought forth a further realization that it could only be truly eased in continued contact with that divine reality which lies in the centre of us all.

It was around this period that she wrote the following:

When I was a child
I used to go and put my face against a tree
The rough and sturdy bark
And the great soaring pillar with its boughs
Comforted me.

Thus, with the fears
And hungers, in the tree's firm embrace,
And childish imaginings,
No shame or grief there was, that tears
Should be wet upon my face.

Oak, larch and pine,
The majesty and glory of the beech,
And the tossing elm —
These have given me strength and absolution
Without act or speech.

Holy be the wood
That in this trestle, dish and chair lives on,
Sturdy, firm and kind,
In beauty and in use we find them good
To lay our dreams upon.

When I was full-grown
I put my hand in his, and leaned my cheek
Upon his cheek. He was kind.
He took my hunger from me, and there was
No need to speak.

You may keep your gems
The dazzling scintillations and allure.
You may keep your gold,
I have a richer treasure in this heart
And a refuge sure.

Tommy did take her hunger from her for a while, as did other men at different stages in her life, but her hunger was never truly satisfied for long. Clare never really found and kept the love she needed from another man, a partner, but she did find it to a greater degree in her relationship with beauty, with truth, with God and indeed she did have 'a richer treasure in her heart and a refuge sure'.

On 26 October 1926 Clare signed an agreement with Cecil Palmer, publishers, 49 Chandos Street, Covent Garden, London WC2 for the sole rights to publishing *Rustle of Spring — Simple Annals of a London Girl* — the memories of her childhood in London's East End. It was published the following year, received considerable attention and was very favourably reviewed in many newspapers and periodicals. In the 10 August 1927 edition of *The Queen* the reviewer spoke of it as being:

> ... the most convincing and moving thing of its sort I have ever read. The author's real name would be warrant for the genuineness of a book that deserves that much abused and overworked term, a human document. Not that any warranty will be needed by anyone who reads even the first few pages of this autobiography of a London girl: daughter of poor parents living somewhere in that region which luckier people vaguely call the East End.
>
> Some of those luckier people have gone from the West End to try to write about life in mean streets. This book is a measure of their failure. It is genuine, done from the inside, with a sincerity that sometimes is almost searing. The pity is that only those who have lived in mean streets, in constant revolt against that sordidness inseparable from poverty in London, will know how true it is. So few who have lived that life can write about it.
>
> But Clare Cameron, as the earliest pages of her autobiography show, was not quite an ordinary child of mean streets. She was ambitious, eager to learn, always reaching out for something better, with that perception of beauty which gives as much pain as pleasure; hungry for books, for music, for friendship, friends who would understand the aspirations and longings which would have seemed so absurd to the family or the neighbours or the relations who came to tea on Sundays. Then the joy of getting work in Fleet Street — that magic street to those who do not know it too well — of earning money and saving up to buy Shelley.
>
> The books we saved up for .... None of the world's masterpieces, no famous book of the moment, acquired more easily in later years, can bring such ecstasy.
>
> It is the note of ecstasy that makes this book alive and true, as much as

Clare Cameron's ruthless analysis, in respect of her miseries and discontents and priggish superiority.

Other reviewers described Clare as being blessed 'with poignant feeling, laying bare the yearnings of a gift of plebeian birth with poetic temperament and nobility of purpose'. 'Clare, the heroine, also knew what beauty meant. She loved art in all its forms — poetry, music, painting; worshipped Nature on the Chingford Hills and yet further afield, and could give reasons for the faith which was in her — although she was born in Bow.' 'She has the soul of a poet, and to give expression in poetry to joyous moments and beautiful thoughts is the breath of life to her.' 'In the end Cinderella joins the elect; Clare's unpretentious story adds another volume to the history of the harassed creative spirit.'

Of the many appreciative letters that Clare received on the publication of her biography she was deeply moved by this one:

Dear Clare Cameron,

Enthusiasm for your book *The Rustle of Spring* compels me to express my sincere appreciation of your individuality. I also know that terrible struggle after Beauty and Truth in the self-same world that you spent your childhood. Perhaps you were slightly more prosperous in your family life than we were, you seem to have been blessed with more copious quantities of "winkles and creeses", and I judge you lived in a whole house, whereas we had never risen above apartments.

And how well I know the chilling rebuke of one's parents in trying to be too big! In your lonely moments of desperation at the drabness of the slums of West Ham, why couldn't it have been me you searched for amongst the passengers at Plaistow Station? I was there, and longing for a kindred spirit.

Your book was so true an expression of my own life, as of course I know it was of yours, that tears happened very frequently. I wonder if we ever rubbed shoulders as we walked along the pavements of Barking Road, Queens Road, Angel Lane, and indeed I know our parents must have in their sojourns at the "Spotted Dog".

Minnie V. King

The realness and vividly descriptive account of Clare's early life in the East End spoke deeply to many hearts and won her greater recognition as a perceptive and sensitive writer. She had the gift of stirring one's hidden feelings; a gift which grew greater and more beautiful through the passage of her years. She had tremendous courage, strength of will and the determination to set full the sails of

Relaxing in Tavistock Square

her strongly built, yet fragile, craft and sail out into the ocean of life.

It was around this time that Clare and Tommy lived in Tavistock Square, London and the late Walford Hyden, Pavlova's conductor, lived with them and drove their car. Amongst many other great artists Clare remembered queuing up to hear Caruso and Melba and seeing Bernhardt and Duse; she also heard the Russian singer Chaliapin. In such company, it was as if some of her deepest hopes and dreams had come true.

Her love of nature grew stronger too; she began to make regular walking tours through different parts of the English countryside and to write of her personal reactions on such trips. She expressed a generous appreciation of the charm of scenery and an eye for the picturesque in people and things, and wrote with an unflagging interest. She wandered far through the most beautiful regions of England and Wales and wrote of each in turn with the same heartfelt delight and devoted rhapsody. Clare often spoke of nature as the mirror of God and in her wanderings she found a peace and delight which she could not find to such a depth in the confines of the city. The beauty of nature inspired and met her need for further creative expression.

Newspapers and periodicals of the time gladly accepted for publication short articles which she wrote about her travels. On 19 December 1928 the *Daily Mail* published the following inspired recollection of some of her explorations:

MY WINTER TRAMPS

Why must the spring and summer in England be the only holiday seasons? Only those who have tramped the countryside in December, and not for a single day but for a number, know what a pleasure and a benefit it can be — how it invigorates body and brain; how richly it adds to the stores of memory.

Instead of huddling over the fire and thinking with a shudder of fog and mud and cold, bare branches and drab landscapes, why not go out and see?

You will be surprised. Put on your thickest boots and underwear. Don't forget your hot-water bottle and flask, and see that your knapsack is really waterproof. Try the Sussex Downs, the Surrey Uplands, or the Chilterns, and if it is too cold on the hills walk around them. The soft colours of earth and sky, if you have eyes to see, will amaze you. There are effects of mist upon still foliage that are never seen in spring or summer; strange vistas in the hushed woods and combes; effects of frost upon twig and leaf, of sun and shadow on the hills, that suggest a world behind the visible world of everyday. You feel a privileged spectator of strange things. I have walked in all seasons and I know.

There is more health in that sharp air that urges you to a brisk four miles an hour and will not let you idle, that expands the lungs, and sharpens the appetite for that delightful fireside tea at dusk. Do you know how good it feels to drop down from the hills to the smoke of the village chimneys, to stretch tired and healthy limbs to the blaze, to light the best cigarette of the day as the frosty stars awake outside? Four days' walking in winter will do you as much good as fourteen in summer.

You will expect to find less comfort, scanty food, unaired beds, and frowns instead of smiles. On the contrary, the stranger who steps into the countryman's winter monotony is doubly welcomed.

There is a big fire as a matter of course, whereas on many a summer evening one shivers because it is not the season for fires. There is abundance of preserves, fruits and vegetables in the store cupboard, since there is only the family to consume it.

Though one receives more attention, charges are considerably less than in the "season". While walking through Sussex last week, in one cottage I was asked 4s. for tea, supper, bed, early tea and breakfast and 3s.6d. in another. In both the food was abundant and of the best country quality and the cosiness and welcome all that could be desired. My last night was spent in a small inn in Surrey, and here for tea, dinner, bed and breakfast and every comfort I was asked 7s.6d.

About this time *The Chronicle* published a reminiscence of a meeting which Clare had with Edward Carpenter, author of *Towards Democracy, Civilisation: Its Cause and Cure* and many other inspired works. It appeared under the title:

A PROPHET OF THE 'CLEARER DAY'

I picked up the slim volume idly. Someone had forgotten it and left it in the hotel lounge. To my pleasure and surprise it was *Towards Democracy*, that brief but passionate paean of freedom of a great man, who died quietly and unsung not so long ago on the outskirts of a growing country town — Edward Carpenter. This was the eighth edition of the little book, whose success over a period of years rivalled the *Leaves of Grass* of his fellow-singer, Walt Whitman. Though I knew much of it by heart I sat down in one of the shabby chairs to taste again the rolling tender phrases, to meet again the warm humanity, the understanding love, the virility and joyousness and appeal of this teacher who in his life as well as in his work was one of the greatest men of his age though in no spectacular sense.

As I put the book aside at last, I recalled the April morning of three years ago when I had overcome my timidity and called on him. From the green track of the Hog's Back, that high ridge of the North Downs which runs from Farnham to Guildford, I had dropped down to the outskirts of that town where he had made his home. For years I had longed to shake the hand of this man, but had been hesitant to intrude. But that morning I summoned the audacity of the ardent disciple and approached the master. I had foolishly expected to find that his home would display something of strangeness; that the patriach and prophet would be living in a hut in the wilderness. Instead I found a neat suburban villa in a hillside street of similar villas. Following my knock I heard footsteps and low voices, and knowing how many people from all over the world visited him every week — some from devotion, some from the less worthy motive of curiosity, or to weary him with banal questions upon his works — I was prepared for disappointment. I had sent no warning of my call, and could hardly expect that he would see me, one of thousands of admirers. But I had forgotten the native courtesy that goes with true greatness.

A man in a baize apron, broad-shouldered, smiling and rose-cheeked, invited me into the small hall, and the tall, slightly-stooping figure of Edward Carpenter approached. I was aware of a slight frame in a well-cut suit, penetrating hazel-eyes crowned by thin, very fine white hair, a

sensitive shaking hand outstretched to greet me, and a gentle questioning voice. For me this was a great moment — the end of a pilgrimage
fulfilled, for here before me at last was the author of two books that had
gladdened, led and sustained me for years, *Towards Democracy* and *Loves
Coming of Age*. The former had been to me a modern Bible, in which I
had found answer to all my problems, and confirmation of my vague
gropings for the truth. Great moments when arrived at last are usually
disappointing, but this was a moment that gave substance to the dream.
For Edward Carpenter did not fail his disciples. Despite the waning
strength of old age — he was then eighty-two — there was in his
presence still that quality that pervaded all his work, a prevailing
sweetness and simplicity, a greatness of heart and soul, that flowed as
easily and naturally about him as those clean airs of Nature that he
loved. There was about him the large, plain sanity that is the mark of all
greatness. It is the reasonableness of Christ and Gautama. All geat
teachers have something of it, and the passage of years cannot efface it.
One received no shock of vivid personality from this gentle figure who
achieved so much. It is not in Nature often to shock or startle or impress,
but to heal and teach and lead us in her ways subtly and almost
imperceptibly, and all his life Carpenter was Nature's child, in the
ordering of his life as well as in spirit.

The hand that waved me to the settee shook, but the gesture was
courtly. I began to talk, quickly and impetuously in my enthusiasm,
forgetting the deafness that hampered him and the sensitive, easily-
flustered nerves of old age. He listened attentively, and laughed deeply
and whole-heartedly at something that amused him. There was nothing
in the cool little sitting room with its plain cream walls, chintzes and
simplicity to suggest the pagan forest, but sitting there on the deep settee
beside him, I felt very much aware of a certain pagan strength and
nobility that nothing of this cheap age had touched.

I felt ashamed of the civilization that had so moulded me that I was
much less clean than he was, so much farther away from the beauty of
living, and the childlike spirit of joy and the real happiness of the soul.
So often the talismans we need the most and travel the world to find, or
seek for years in the wide fields of knowledge or the intricacies of our
own thoughts, talismans of content and illumination, lie beneath the
nearest stones, so near that our hurried feet have passed over them long
ago, and it has not occurred to us to give a backward glance. Carpenter
never hurried, never dimmed the clear pool of his mind with a scum of
useless knowledge. One feels that he knew many secrets that are hidden
from us, secrets that are secrets no longer to those who carry that
simplicity and meekness and intuition, which, untouched by manners
and modes, sees God and inherits the earth. For Carpenter's God was
not of the churches and creeds, but that wider, all-embracing spirit that

expresses itself in trees and stars and the ever-renewing earth, in air and
fire and water and the soul of man, in love and aspiration and art; that
thin, pure flame which the churches strangle and confine and distort, but
which alone is the Way, the Truth, and Life. He spoke of this cabined
and limited Christianity in a tone of kindly tolerance as his eyes looked
beyond, as he told me of that long time of spiritual upheaval which
preceded *Towards Democracy*, and the mental stress under which it was
written.

There have been few men who have so blended in their personalities
and their work such perfect balance of body, mind and spirit.

There was a branch of fading mimosa in the window and the
casement curtains were blowing in the wind. One might have passed the
tall figure with the uncertain steps often along the sunny road, and not
known that one had seen the prophet of that clearer day we call the
Millenium, and who will be remembered among the Immortals. For
there was nothing sensational or striking about Edward Carpenter,
except that inherent nobility which so easily passes unnoticed.

His message was delivered many years ago and recognised and hailed
by many; his work is done, and many are his followers. But in this
restless, mechanical and commercial age we seem very little nearer that
new Democracy to which he has tried to lead us, the democracy of the
spirit that leads to the only true and abiding democracy of fact.

A chill wind, common to the early English Spring, met me at the
garden gate. It was very like the seeking soul of man, blown hither and
thither in search of satisfaction and aim. Yet here, in the teaching of this
man who was neither ascetic nor saint, but the child of Pan and men as
well as God, the way may still be found. If Carpenter's message be
studied and employed, then, and then only will there be peace in our
time.

In 1930 Constable published *Green Fields of England*, a book of
footpath travels by Clare, and described by a reviewer: 'True
pictures of the quiet countryside under the glowing summer sun are
reflected throughout the pages of this book. It is a delightful, vividly
descriptive volume to be read and pondered and placed among the
library treasures.'

Many supportive and complimentary reviews followed its publication and she was described as a 'sister-in-art' to Richard Jefferies
and Edward Thomas and called 'brilliantly successful in capturing
the charm of the English countryside in all its many moods'. In
Green Fields of England Clare painted a series of pictures in words
which vividly recalled places seen and known and encouraged the
reader to discover the beauty and inspiration to be found in such

places when one wanders with the heart of an explorer, the eye of an artist and the pen of a poet. Through her un-clouded and expansive perception she presented to the seeking mind an observant eye and a por-trayal of the beauty, graciousness and peace of the countryside. She also supplied much practical information for the way-farer about many of the old English inns, also appealing to the student of history. She divided the chapters of the book by some of her poems; of the nine that are included my favourite is:

Setting out on a walking tour

DISCONSOLATE LUNCHEON

About the table silver-spread
They talked of servants and of bills,
Of friends and foes, the live, the dead,
Across the bowls of daffodils.

Through secret crevice of the mind,
Behind my social smiling eyes,
My spirit fled into the kind
And lovely far-flung sanctuaries ....

'A sad affair!' I heard one say,
And made my ready Yes and No,
But I was singing far away
And running where the wild deer go.

But I was gathered to my lord,
My lord the sun; on summit high
I laughed to see his flashing sword
Smiting coloured earth and sky.

But I was gathered where I stood
With beasts four-footed, nymph and faun,
They ran to meet me through the wood,
Satyr, sprite and leprechaun.

I took their hands and danced with them,
And all the earth was ours for play.
O sweet escape from world of men,
O light immortal on the day!

We were so happy long ago,
My brothers of the sun and wind,
Uplifted far from earthly woe,
Hands in loving hands entwined.

We were so happy long ago,
On sunlit shore, in scented fern;
Come day of joy, when I shall know
That from you there is no return ....

They talked in level tones and grey
Of this and that, and so and so ....
But I was singing far away
And running where the wild deer go.

In the chapter on Sussex she wrote of the stream she loved best at
Maresfield:

... a most humble little brook by a green track that ran into the woods at
Piltdown. The path thereto is not far from the road, but once upon it
one is embraced by a solitude and quiet that is the legacy of the centuries.
In a moment of time the world and the period is forgotten and sunny
Arcadia beckons. Perhaps it was that recognition, which is love at first
sight, that brought the throb to the blood the first day I walked there.
There was severance as well as excitement in my fingers as they opened
the farmyard gate, as I passed along the meadow's edge and round by
the coppice to what sweet discoveries I knew not. By the farm, and
spaciously set, a great stone barn stands upon the sky. Behind it tosses a
line of noble, wind-blown pines, that upon that first morning acquaintance, burned upon the deep blue sky with the ardour of crusaders. Has
no artist ever discovered that grey barn with its line of soaring trees?
The track goes through windy fields, and skirts a hedge where the

primroses wink from the hollow, past a wood where pheasants and partridge rise startled from the mysterious brake. A square grey house with mullioned windows stands at the meadow's corner, with an old mill-stone sunk in the turf below it. The facing woods draw closer, there is sight of a little bridge, and the pulses quicken as one comes nearer to the music of the water. Such a little brook it was, curving under banks of anemones and wild daffodils, and the exploration of the wild duck. I cannot say why it sang of Greece and the Golden Age, for it was like many other little brooks. There upon its green banks in the sunny solitude of a hot morning, two who had been acquaintances met as friends, and knew that simple lyric happiness in the hour and in themselves of which none have truly sung but Theocritus, and he but faintly. For such things are spun of leaves and wings, and scent and air and water, and of the curious fluttering spirit hidden in the clay. We have no means of telling them. The brook is there no longer, but has been flooded to a lake that spreads clear wide on either hand of the green path for the nurturing of trout and wild-fowl. The scene is very beautiful there now, and I do not miss the stream, which has vanished as all beautiful things must, soon or late, and which babbled for me so sweet a swan-song close upon its passing. In memory it has immortal life.

Here on a breezy morning, I lingered to drink in the fair picture of the blowing ash tree and the green land rising against the milky sky, before wandering on to the clearing where the primroses starred the leaves so thickly that the woodland floor was indeed a carpet. The happy child there plucking primroses alone in the windy morning, with the doves crooning in the trees above, will never forget the pleasure of that hour, the simple and perfect joy that was tearful behind the eyes.

Here, too, I lay alone one long golden afternoon, rapt on the breast of earth and drowsed by the singing water, until the very sky seemed to lean down and gather me to its arms. Here on all these times I knew revelation and joy, and cannot tell for which of them I love the singing water of the little brook. But, because of these things, the beautiful and perfect hours lifted out of life, the green bank there will be for ever a blest and happy place .... The woods beyond have a quality like no other woods. The trees there, mostly birch and beech and alder, are young trees, and the pale sun of April glinting on the brambles and the lichens, spun a sweet and silver light. Nymphs must once have known the place, and Pan piped out thin melody from the foot of a slender tree. It seemed that as we walked the narrow path upon that drowsy afternoon the birds of the air and the beasts of the field, the spirits that live in the trees and in the shadowy places, came out and walked with us. We were in the midst of a great company, as in the midst of a glad and mighty music. How many words tell of the privilege and the high estates of that hour, of the sense of eternal youth in the heart and eternal peace in the soul? How shall I tell of the love and the recognition that came from the young trees and the birds in the boughs, from all His creatures near and far, from the sunshine and the very air, so that we were lifted for a space from the world into the glory of the Kingdom of Heaven? My faith bows down as I recall that silver wood, and the blessing of God that encompassed us there, for if earthly life hereafter is forever grey, there is courage and comfort unutterable in the memory of that hour, in its shining promise of immortality.

Born in very ordinary circumstances in conditions that could easily have stifled her perceptive and creative spirit, there was an unquenchable thirst within Clare that drove her on to seek that wondrous well of water that lies hidden beyond the mundane and the tinsel of life. Her poems and writings echoed more and more the radiance and music of eternity, singing through the beauties of nature, through the heart of each and every one of us, as it has done before time began and will do forever. Her thoughts and way of seeing things bore evidence of the natural mystic she was and her memory of a heavenly state of consciousness, present with her since birth, awakened in those who read her writings a perception akin to the depth of her own awareness. Later on, she spoke of her mystical experiences since childhood and of the wisdom that is constantly taught by Mother Earth.

In chapter one of *Green Fields of England* she said:

I hope they are not many, those who have no secret garden of the mind. For this garden alone can give refreshment when life is barren of peace or sustenance or satisfactory answer. Such sanctuaries may be reached by a certain philosophy or faith, by the guidance of a beloved author or an understanding friend, by way of the temples of music and art, or by groping after truth through the vast kingdoms of knowledge. They encompass almost always truth and beauty, and are radiant with the light that never was on sea or land.

But they are not always to be found by seeking; often one stumbles upon them with the suddenness of unexpected shock. The spirit bows down and worships them, aware of unworthiness, faltering its recognition and its praise.

One reader who was very impressed with this volume wrote to Clare, saying:

You have written a beautiful book — you are a poet and an artist — it is refreshing to read such a book, out of the spate of so-called modern literature ... the most delightful, soul-satisfying book that I, personally, have come across this year ....

I find the style of your writing exactly right. I hate gush and fine writing; there is nothing of that objectionable quality in yours. You write from the heart and not the head, and express yourself in every line, without the slightest appearance of effort, with simple sincerity. And as you have always something real and true to say, and very real powers of expression, the result is most happy. I find your simple poetic prose very charming, worthy of reading aloud for the sheer music of it.

Your poetry is as attractive as your prose, and I shall look forward to the next book you publish.

As it happens I have visited nearly all the places you mention in your book, either on foot or, in the old days, bicycling. I often still take my bicycle for a walk, across country, over field and woodland, anywhere and everywhere. I call it tramp-cycling — the roads being impossible nowadays.

Although I have a car I am still of opinion that the pleasantest form of locomotion, and the *only* way of seeing England properly, is on foot by field paths .... I find that the older one gets the more one loves the quiet places, and simple people. It is only be seeking them that one finds reality. I congratulate you; you have got your values right. That is what we are here for, I believe.

A book like yours makes one thank God that there are still right-minded, sane people in England. Youth and poets may save our country yet!

In the summer of 1931 Wakefield Central School in East Ham, which Clare attended from 1910-13, celebrated the twenty-first anniversary of its opening and in the *East Ham Echo* of 24 July the following reference to Clare appeared:

Wakefield Central School has just celebrated its "coming of age", and it is with a very real sense of pleasure that we offer our congratulations to this famous East Ham school. During its long career, "Wakefield" has maintained high tradition, and many students, passing out to the wider world, have gained further laurels to add to the distinction of their alma mater.

One of "Wakefield's" old scholars is the wife of Mr. Thomas Burke, the famous writer of Limehouse life. She is herself an authoress with a large following of readers. Not all the scholars can claim to have attained such heights but even in the present "first year" there are many whose ambitions are as lofty.

In the same year she contributed to the series of brochures on British inns, published by the True Temperance Association. Her

article on the Luttrell Arms, Dunster, on the Taunton and Bridg-
water road was well acclaimed by the critics because of her beautiful
and historic description of it:

> ... It has known many kinds of history, ecclesiastic, domestic, military,
> and their savours linger still about the old walls and rafters, distilled into
> the essence of the past. Many and strange and infinitely various have
> been the figures that have passed beneath its porch. Many are but the
> shades of conjecture, for not yet is its story fully known, or all its
> legends told. But that perhaps is part of its charm. Its dignity, vigorous
> and appealing still, will remain, while stone clings to stone, an admirable
> corrective to the hasty careless life which in summer passes its door or
> crosses its threshold. Hence there is food for the spirit as well as the
> enquiring mind and hungry inner man, in this one of the finest of our
> English inns, of which we may be justly proud.

Both Tommy and Clare shared a love for old English inns.
Tommy wrote a number of popular books on various inns and on
different parts of England — in this aspect they shared a keen
interest. Clare retained her love for old inns right up until she died
and often would remark that people were closer to each other in
pubs than they were in some churches!

She was very much an individual and wrote about what she
believed. In *The Woman's View* — a quarterly issue, in January
1932, she wrote an enquiry on equality:

> This is not a plea for the rights of women, for apart from the fact that this
> object is considered to have been achieved long ago, the subject arouses
> that stupid antagonism which leads nowhere. It is a plea for a recog-
> nition of a common need, a re-statement of values. Briefly, it may be
> summarised thus. I am tired of that rough classification which, in an age
> which considers itself honest and emancipated, still in every discussion
> of every subject sharply divides human beings into men and women,
> like the sheep and the goats, irrespective of the fact that they are first of
> all individuals and must behave as such, irrespective of the fact that they
> become more and more like each other every day. They lead similar
> lives, suffer the same hungers and thirsts of body, mind and spirit, the
> same conflicts and embarrassments and difficulties, and reveal the same
> social needs. A few of these, once considered shameful or indecent or
> unladylike, and inconsistent with the old sentimental idea of Woman,
> have been honestly recognised, but there are many gaps yet.
> ... I happen to walk alone a great deal about the English countryside.
> I like to prowl about London also alone. For not only by nature am I a
> solitary, but consider that only thus can one properly observe, and catch

Tramping in Provence with two journalists,
just before the war

the atmosphere either of city, village, or tract of countryside. But I am also shy, young, and rather timid, and consequently embarrassed when I attract attention, or appear to be doing anything which by written or unwritten law I ought not. Like most other human creatures when taking long exercise in the open air, I want refreshment in the middle of the day. I do not always want lunch, nor even the traditional bread and cheese. But often when passing through small villages which possess but one small inn apiece, I have gone thirsty rather than face the sudden silence which falls upon the loud and cheerful tap-room when a strange "young lady" enters. I have passed the larger hotel also, because of my memories of barmaids who look askance at the girl in the rough tweeds when she sought the reviving Guinness, because of my diffidence in entering a lounge full of farmers or sportsmen. Despite the fact that women fly alone to the ends of the earth nowadays and that all roads and occupations are open to them, I am unpleasantly conscious of the fact that still I feel an intruder when I enter alone the average saloon-bar. It is the same at night. After dinner, in that relaxed mood which hankers for human society, I am shown the drawing room, upon whose usually frigid atmosphere I need make no comment. Not for a woman is the genial bar or smoke-room below, with its flow of easy talk and odd encounter. On these many occasions, when my timid spirit compels me to observe the proprieties, I have longed for the day when the sexes shall no longer be so differentiated, but considered members of the same human family. I hope then it will be recognised that their sometimes widely-differing tastes and eccentricities derive from the fact that they are *individuals*, not necessarily because they are either men or woman, and therefore expected to behave according to category.

... What is called for is the beginning of a woman's movement which shall develop a cafe-bar along her own lines, an unobtrusive place which refrains from being either Bohemian or arty or prim, but which shall satisfy the needs of most women. It shall be a place where men are welcomed gladly, but which will remain primarily her concern, as the average public-house is man's today. With her emancipation and increasing equality with men, she has every right to be taken seriously about it. As she shares his work and his play I hope she may share his relaxations. Most of them she does, and it will be retorted cynically that already she shares his tavern as she shares his club. But I fear it will be a long time yet before she is admitted there simply and naturally as a human creature, with the same kind of social hunger which the drawing room, the restaurant, the theatre do not always satisfy. This I consider is sufficient justification for an effort on her own behalf.

... What is wanted is the recognition of the fact that she needs and has earned not only an unquestioning admittance to one of man's strongholds, but one of her own which shall raise the standard of the English inns still higher. With her entry into a comparatively new field, her increasing interest and work for its improvement and public recognition thereof, there is no limit to the social possibilities of one of the oldest English institutions, and its power for good. Which brings me back to my original plea. May one hope soon there will be less talk of men and women and what is expected of each of them, and more of human beings? Less antagonism, and more sympathy and understanding. Only then will it be realised that we are once again slowly approaching the old godlike state of Man, who was neither man or woman but both in one creature. And in those days all men upon earth were friends.

Other articles by Clare appeared in national newspapers that year. They laid particular emphasis on the individuality and recognition of woman in her own right and of the needs of mind and spirit as well as of the body of woman being met before the harmonious balance of the full rich life could be achieved.

At this time Clare was also reading books on philosophy; alternative ways of healing; mysticism; Eastern wisdom and other writings on the deeper meaning and purpose of life. Some of the writers whose works had a lasting impression on her were: Walt Whitman, George Russell, Kahlil Gibran, Algernon Blackwood, Helen Waddell, John Cowper Powys, Edward Carpenter and Arthur

Clare with her parents and brother, East Ham, 1934

Machen; in addition, she explored *The Tibetan Book of the Dead*, *The Secret of the Golden Flower*, *The Tao Te Ching* and other such classics.

She began to realize, further, the necessity for humility, simplicity, surrender; making room for the knowledge of the soul; and the validity of expanding awareness into the universal consciousness, transcending the personal level which imprisons and deceives us. She hungered after a greater experience of the unity underlying everything, that relates everyone and everything where nothing is separate and no man is an island though he may feel one. More and more she was discovering the importance of the abiding truths of eternity and the embodiment of these truths in one's daily life.

Her search for these deeper truths led her to the study of Buddhism which has moulded the life of much of the Eastern world. Little did she realize beforehand what the effect of this religion-philosophy would have in moulding the next twelve years or so of her life.

3

The War Years
and the Buddha

Clare's interest in Buddhism strengthened and grew. She became close friends with Christmas Humphreys, a judge and founder of the Buddhist Society in England and she was involved in the Society's activities which were then run from a little house in South Eaton Place, London. Alan Watts was at this time editor of *Buddhism in England* and when he went to the USA with his bride in 1938 Clare took over the editorship.

In the short time which Clare knew Alan Watts she became very fond of him. He was a remarkable young man who, at the age of nineteen, wrote one of the best books on Zen by a Westerner, *The Spirit of Zen*, which was published by John Murray in their 'Wisdom of the East' series. He later became a well-known lecturer and author, particularly in America, and wrote many more books on Zen Buddhism and the Zen way of life. Before he left England he gave Clare a signed painting by himself depicting an old Zen monk riding an ox who, having found a lost animal (his lost "self") and bringing it under control, returns home peacefully seated upon it. This much-appreciated gift always remained a treasure to Clare and she left it with me when she died. It continues to grace the wall here in my home at Bosham House.

When the Buddhist headquarters in Eaton Place was bombed during the Second World War Clare found them two rooms on the first floor of 106 Great Russell Street, WC1. For the next ten years she played a large part in the expansion of the journal and of the Society, giving numerous talks and helping Buddhism to become more widely known in England.

Her friendship with Christmas Humphreys remained for the rest of her life. 'Toby', as she affectionately knew him, helped and encouraged Clare in her work with the Buddhist Society and in her personal life. They both shared a characteristic zeal to get things going; to be catalysts; to be open-minded and wholeheartedly to embrace Eastern religious ideas, not generally so readily accepted as they are today.

With the re-organization of the Society, *Buddhism in England* became *The Middle Way* and it remains so-called today, appearing quarterly from the present Buddhist Society headquarters at 58 Eccleston Square, London SW1. During this period in Clare's life she wrote profusely. As well as her editorials, she continued to give talks on Buddhism and also instigated the Foundations of Peace Series which consisted of a number of booklets on the theme of peace, most apt in those war-torn days. In *The Way of Becoming* (No. 3 Foundations of Peace Series) Clare wrote:

> The Way of Becoming may be compared not only to the wheel of balanced forces, ceaselessly and smoothly revolved through all exper- ience, not only to the spiral of growth where those forces are purified and transmuted from the gross to the fine, but also to a star whose rays are infinite. Not for scenic reasons does the star appear so frequently in myth, legend and scripture. Ever in motion with a dynamic con- centrated life, it is a shining wheel. The luminosity comes from the movement towards purification. It is also the emanation of wisdom, joy and love. There is no wisdom, joy or love without this "shining". But wherever there is conflict, maladjustment, fear, disease, there will be patches of darkness. The movement is blocked there, or operates in spasmodic jerks. As a result we are restless, dissatisfied, unhappy. In the majority of us, this ignorance is mixed with our enlightenment, and discord with harmony, as dust covers a mirror. Let us return to the Steps of the Noble Eightfold Path (Right Understanding, Right Motive, Right Speech, Right Action, Right Livelihood, Right Discrimination, Right Concentration and Right Meditation), considering them not only as the spokes of the wheel of the psyche, but as rays of the stars. Although we read of them as separate, in sequence, they are not really so. They are described as such because mental interpretations of truth must be stretched out in a line of words to match the reactions of our eyes and thoughts. Our mental mechanism can take in only one viewpoint at a time, which is sufficient commentary on the limited nature of thought! The Steps of the Noble Eightfold Path are inter- penetrating sections of one whole, and work harmoniously *only* as a whole. For example, if you think about it a little, you will find that all steps are contained in each step. If one is neglected, the others are undernourished or put out of alignment accordingly.

Therefore, our primary and essential aim should be towards this unity. Not straining to achieve in one direction, with the impatience and sense of futility it often implies. Such a conception of the Path is confined to spatial and dimensional limits, and as such is an illusion which it is our endeavour to transcend. We shall never transcend it while we stay *in* it. At first, therefore, we must be at peace with ourselves, content to grow slowly in all fields of our expression, denying none and affirming the inherent spiritual nature of all. A man at peace with himself is at peace with the universe. It is not a static complacency, but a dynamic recognition of the Way of Becoming. In this sense, all life "becomes", from the lesser to the greater, the simple to the complex, from the finite to the infinite.

Our nature is boundless. We do not yet know what we may become. The paths which we take now, unifying them deliberately, are as a model of the greater creation we perform superconsciously. For when paths are united, we find that the gates (complexes and barriers to understanding) open of themselves. When paths are united, how wide is the road! How unconfined, free and light-hearted we feel as we take it! When the little flames of our various aspirations are united, how great is the light! Much that was obscure to us, that we saw in part, now becomes clear because we begin to see the whole. Much that we isolated (i.e., one desire at war with another desire), futile (because we could not attain our personal ends), and meaningless (because the intuition was not awakened within us) now takes its place in significance and purpose. And in that light, that peace, that freedom, we see our fellow-travellers. We were too concerned with egotistic ends to see them before. How interesting they all are, how lovable! How piteous, tragic, noble is this Ever-becoming of which we are a part! All life is one. To realise it, we must feel ourselves as one, where all the striving 'selves' in us make friends, and thus gladly co-operate in serving That which they love, That to which they belong. Then we are naturally friends with all men, with all sentient life. They are externalised projections, continuations, of all the multiple selves contained in us. What we have been, are and shall be, they are in the Eternal Now, where past, present, and future are interpenetrating sections of the whole.

All is contained in the great wheel, in the spiral and the star. Surely it is good and wise and lovely to find this Way within, of which these three are living symbols. Surely it is good, wise and lovely to want to awaken it, learn its wonderful laws and set it moving in harmonious control.

Why do we remain in ignorance of it, preferring darkness to light, disorder to order, struggle to peace, when the practical teaching of the Buddha is laid as an open book before us? One reason only. "You yourselves must make the effort. Buddhas do but point the Way."*

* With kind permission of the Buddhist Society.

Clare's involvement with Buddhism developed out of her yearning to embrace the application of universal and timeless truths unattached to specifically Buddhist teaching. At this period in her life, though, she found herself particularly in tune with the Buddhist Way:

> Such is the need of the hour, that need can be understood, accepted and met only through personal dedication and experience, by taking our part in bringing the new era to birth.
>
>   It is by the orientation of the heart and the practical application of our realisations, in whatsoever walk of life we find ourselves and whatever creed we profess (or none), that this will come to pass. For then with every breath, word and act, we shall be giving forth the Buddhist salutation:
>
> Peace to All Beings

With the trauma, conflict and fear in those war days very evident in London; the bombings; the loss of loved ones and the rapid change — these very factors drove many people to establish a deeper faith and build stronger foundations within themselves as the present structure crumbled. For Clare, Buddhism had a lot to offer in those troubled days. Its teaching of love, compassion and the unity of living things was very close to Clare's heart. In the Buddhist belief the evolving consciousness achieves successive states of spiritual achievement through many lives, until Buddhahood is reached. Only then is the self entirely dead and the Great Self (God self) released from its bondage, merging as a dewdrop into the shining sea, the source of all life.

Gautama the Buddha, the awakened one, brought the knowledge of eternal truths to the East as did Jesus Christ to the West. His teaching of the Middle Way struck a deep chord in Clare's soul. In the early 1940s she wrote of the Middle Way in *The Flowing Stream*, a selection of her editorials from the *Buddhist Journal*:

> It is not there, but here. It is beyond all conditions, and it is in the midst of conditions. It is an open book, but there is nothing written on its pages. For to look for it "there" is to look for something other than its essential Nature. To run forth to grasp, whether a possession, the ladder of an ideal, the comfort of a friend, or the refuge of a doctrine, is to fall into the Heresy of Separateness, to be subject to vicarious atonement, to lose the Way. All that is our own will come to us, perpetually comes to us. Take nothing, and you will receive all.
>
>   There is a possession. Enjoy it. And when it dissolves, as it will, your

hand will not beat the air in frustration. For you will have learned to let everything be, and go. In any case, another possession is on the way (unless you shut the door in its face, lest it hurt you) and within the husk of each, as it breaks, is the sweet kernel of experience that nourishes the soul.

There is the ideal, with manifold ladders. How we pant and climb, straining towards the fugitive vision, reaching not for a gross and concrete possession like our brother materialist, but an abstract and lofty one. Let go of all ladders! You have wings. Only when you have ceased to strive for attainment will you know that attainment is already quickening within you. But then you will not give it a name.

The friend advises, cheers and sustains you on the plains. On the mountain slopes you call for him, and he is not there. It is the place of the One, not the many; of the Unified, not the separate. How cold is the air, but clear. You can see, after the obscurity of valley mists. How empty the solitude, but how boundless, free and still, after the clutter, confusion and clamour that you knew below! And in that expansion and raising of consciousness there is your friend, known as never before, and likewise supported. How can you need each other in this place where all needs — having been relinquished — are fulfilled? For the first time perhaps you love him, not with your flesh, but with your spirit. For you are face to face, "in the spirit". We have vowed to take refuge in the Doctrine. What is the Doctrine? Is it a book, a code, a religion? These are means, not ends. Let us beware that, by holding them up before us, they do not obscure the Light! The Doctrine is the Way to Eternal Life, for which we *lay down* the book, the code, the religion. Then they become roads, whereby and whereupon we pass into the fuller realisation of Life, using them, but unimpeded, clinging to nothing, having nothing, free. Almost one might say, going nowhere. No "where". For it is here, not manifest but potential, in the midst of conditions. It is within, where already "thou art Buddha".

It is an open book, but all that assertive will, the greedy desire, the artfulness of the monkey mind would write is erased from its pages. For they have no place in Eternal Life.

Seek but to become the pure and pristine page, and Divinity, thus released from the fetters of illusion within you, will write the invisible script. And it is That for which you have become the channel that others will read, by what you are.

The Middle Way hears no footfall, leaves no footprint. It is the Way of the free, the unburdened, the selfless, the pure in heart. Let us learn to tread it.

Those turbulent years were fraught with difficulties. Clare never knew when another bombing raid would happen, where a street would be blocked with the results of another explosion or at times where she would sleep or how much longer she would live. The then Poet Laureate, John Masefield, was a subscriber to *Buddhism in England*, a poet whose verses resonated with the depths of Clare's own poetic nature.

The war sounded the note of responsibility, of which Clare stated at the time:

> All life is one. As a large part of Europe disintegrates in flames, though we may not feel it to be so, yet in some degree we are responsible. There are no sharp divisions between the individual, national and world karma. As Europe rises again phoenix-like from the ashes, we are responsible.
>
> We are responsible whether playing leading or minor parts, active in battle or engaged in occupations of peace on "the home front". For by our general attitude we contribute something to the exaltation or degradation of life every moment, to its movement forward or backward, or to its stagnation. By what we are we aid the liberation of light from the present darkness, order from chaos, or impede it. There is no escape from this responsibility in indifference, in bewilderment before the vast complexity of the situation which is beyond the comprehension and solution of most of us. Hatred ceaseth not by hatred, but only by love. From the larger point of view a petty spite, a trifling greed, some minor urge to power are as potent at this time as military operations, which, indeed, they are in embryo. They are on the wrong side of the scale at a time when the spiritual freedom of men (as distinct from the physical) hangs in the balance.
>
> All life is one. We canalise these aspects of it to which we relate ourselves. According to the quality of our reactions, we become expressions for the universal forces, from the sublime to the debased, and all the degrees between. Hence love at its most selfless, pure and devoted, by law of attraction, is fed from the Source of Love, protected by Love and guided by Love. It will be effective in its manifestation according to its distance from the Source, which is dependent on its quality. Serenity, fearlessness and compassion will be maintained according to our steadfast allegiance to the Source of Peace deep within, however often we are tempted to forsake it by the impact of external phenomena. We shall see truly and act rightly in so far as we make room for Truth to manifest through us, not now and again, but every moment.
>
> These few examples of daily exercises in practical Buddhism are within the reach of all, but they will not be found possible on the inflamed and scarred circumference of our lives unless we are related to the inner centre. There alone is the inspiring, motivating and sustaining

power. Hence the need for the cultivation of the spiritual life through meditation was never more urgent than it is today. It is easy to cherish the ideals, but we may not by-pass our responsibilities, but clear the way for the embodiment of such ideals. The work begins when we know just what we are contributing, and in the future are prepared to contribute, to the degeneration or regeneration of the world.

As well as her writings on Buddhism Clare continued to write her poetry. Christmas 1941 gave birth to:

THE RHYTHM

Very long is the night
As we ride over the rim of the turning world
Into the veiled unknown;
And so hooded our sight
That every man in his cloak of silence
Broods, or dreams, or wages war in his heart
Confused, alone.

Yet somewhere far, or near,
The day is breaking in summer and shining air.
How few in the darkness know ...
Or see the clear
Track under the hooves; and feel the star-ringed fingers
Lightly laid on the frosty bridles, leading
The way we go.

It is not long till day.
The world will swing from shadow to the sun.
And wars, bereft of power,
With dreams will drift away,
And lifting up our heads, we shall smile to waken.
I will take your hand and bid you
Good-morning in that hour,

As we ride over the rim of the turning world
Breaking into flower.

In 1942 Clare privately printed a book of poems, *A Stranger Here*, which met with a most encouraging reception at the hands of the leading critics. *John O'London's Weekly* described her free verse as being 'tighter, almost metrical, and her conventional verse is of classical finish and flavour. Pastoral, religious and meditative, often profound, and sometimes truly mystical....' *The Times Literary Supplement* in its press notice said: 'Eastern wisdom is felt, not as a doctrine, but as something which has been absorbed by her sensibility to which it gives depth and meaning, in her immediate response to flowers or trees.' The title of the book sprung from the depths of Clare's heart, that this world is not our true habitat, but we belong to that better country where decay is unknown and flowers never fade. Upon reading these vividly descriptive poems, in a receptive and understanding mood, one becomes conscious of the conflict and the struggle that was going on in the depths of her soul; the labour pains that preceded the birth of the poems:

THE COMFORTER

When querulous I am confined
In dark illusions of the mind,
Or unhappy and frustrate
Cry out on circumstance and fate —
If Beauty can but come to me
Her hand alone shall set me free.

A yellowing branch, in autumn dress'd
Upon the blue sky's palimpsest,
Or leafless, and its portrait thrown
By sun at noon on ivory stone —
These unlock the iron and frost
Without effort, without cost.

So soft her touch, surprising, swift,
Fugitive through shadow's rift,
Yet leaps my heart to see her wings
Angelic over common things.
And so this day, in wall and tree,
Beauty gave her hand to me.

THE CROWN

When sap was low, and subtle thieves
Had stripped me of my sheltering leaves,
And black and harsh as any stone
My wintered spirit stood alone,
I stretched my hand, with upturned palm,
In dumb desire for beauty's balm.

When I went forth, with lifted head,
I saw how trees, that late were dead,
Now bore on upturned branch and bough

Their flowers and coronals of snow,
And I laughed, for to atone,
For that poor fool, who had not known.

During this time Clare and Tommy lived in Queensway. Recent years had brought Tommy further fame with the publication of a stream of books on London, English inns and the English country-side; also short stories and many articles in leading newspapers and magazines. To Thomas Burke's mind the hurly-burly of London life provided him with the stimulant to his imagination which, as a writer, he needed. Recent titles from his pen included: *Living in Bloomsbury*; *Abduction*; *The Streets of London* and *English Night Life*. He was a man of integrity in his speech, his life and in his books; it was that which made him the fine and fastidious writer he was and, though their ways differed, Tommy and Clare continued to share their aspirations as writers and their love for each other.

Clare continued lecturing and writing essays on Buddhism. After a conversation which Clare had with Christmas Humphreys on a morning in May, 1943, he wrote to her later that same day:

How few understand the Passion of God. When I read and hear things stated something in me weeps for there is not the slightest acknow-ledgement of Him, or very little. For if there were, the readings of what had been written would *move* people whereas all that happens is that they are entertained or mentally stimulated. True it is, that many would resent things written and said but it would only be those unhealed and unsurrendered areas of consciousness. Those arrogant rebellions which have become chrystallised. The very being of man is divine. Full of divine potency. He does not have to evolve, as ordinarily understood. *He* has to become *what he already is*. Through allowing God to have His way with him. And what a way it is. How tender He is. How gracious. How full of compassion. How lovely in His unceasing ministry unto us even when we are most opposed to Him. He changes not nor fails. Nor ever could. For it is He, is it not?

And shall our ways become like His ways. So that even our mental atmospheres are not an offence against our fellow-man. So that the very streams of our emotion shall become as the Balm of Gilead. And the radiation of His Presence within us shall remove every unclean element from us, so that, as we walk, we shall be as a benediction unto all whom we meet in the way....

Toby
(Christmas Humphreys)

Through the avenue of her poetry in particular, the radiance of God's presence, of truth and beauty flowed like sparkling, unadulterated water from an underground spring in Clare's heart. In 1944 she privately published another collection of her poems titled *Far from Home*; this contained more evocative and mystical verse full of beauty and a depth of understanding which again brought inspiration and comfort to the reader:

THE ETERNAL QUEST

I sought for Thee within the secret gardens
That men find fair upon the painted earth,
I lifted many a sable cloak to find Thee
Within the eyes of pain, upon the lips of mirth.

I felt Thy touch in hands of friends and brothers,
And burned for Thee in Love's sharp sweet embrace,
Ah, surely there and then the mists were riven
Upon the flashing glory of Thy face!

I bowed in the inner tower of silence,
And faintly heard Thy voice upon the air.
In solitude Thou didst companion me, and never
Was companion or lover more terrible and fair.

But I may not keep Thee, nor come nearer,
Though deep within my being I explore.
Beyond the deepest dark, the transcendental
Aflame Thou art beyond the farthest door.

My heart is sick with hunger, my Beloved,
For long ago in kingdoms of the Sun,
Beyond the shores of Truth and Love and Beauty
When there was neither Thee nor Me, but One.

THE OCEAN

I yield myself unto Thy Sea
In all its vast immensity.
Buried deep its secret floor;
Immeasurably far the shore.

Like organ notes the breakers roll
In thunder now about the soul,
This fragile little ship that rides
The mighty rhythm of the tides.

> The hours a slow processional weave
> From dazzling day to starry eve,
> With Thy Mystery rich and full,
> Majestic, measured, beautiful.
>
> Nought is here, but sea and sky,
> None, my God but Thou and I.
> Tossed beyond all time and space
> Thou hast met me, face to face.
>
> It is enough! For I am free
> Upon the music of Thy Sea.
> My feet have touched its secret floor,
> My arms stretch to the distant shore,
>
> And none shall bind me evermore.

On 22 September 1945 Thomas Burke died of peritonitis at the Homeopathic Hospital, Great Ormond Street, London. Tommy had been ill for some years and the only journeys that he had been able to make in the years prior to his death were to the London Library. He wrote *The Streets of London*, *English Night Life*, *Travel in England* and *The English Townsman* while a sick man and most of them while the bombs were falling on London. The war years impinged on his sensitive and very highly strung temperament. Clare supported him through his years of ill-health and admired his courage in accepting responsibility when not fitted for it. Later, when speaking of Tommy, Clare described him:

> He was apt to be shy, and gave the impression to strangers of withdrawal. But in the right company he was an excellent conversationalist. His chief interests were browsing in his library, listening to music, and intelligent conversation. His ideas were sufficiently original and spirited to shock the mediocre, and to the last he remained a rebel against all standardisation, mechanisation, and the current trend of regimentation. He had no use for cant and humbug, and expressed it forcibly; his sense of values and proportion were refreshingly sane and sound, and at no time did he follow the fashion, either in literature or life. He was also a poet and philosopher.

Their relationship over the years had had its difficulties and Clare's inherent passion for change and adventure resulted in her being unfaithful on a few occasions. All of Tommy's energy went into his writing and, when he became impotent, Clare sought sexual fulfilment through other lovers with whom she shared a close relationship. She humbly reflected on her failings in this respect in later years and confessed to being very human. The several affairs which she had outside the marriage did not change the deep fondness which she had for Tommy, nor his fondness for her.

While in hospital, just before he died, Tommy wrote Clare the following note:

My Dear,

I hope you may have an easy and tranquil two or three days to yourself. You have earned it after all the bother you've had over me and I do appreciate all that you've done and the present nuisance of breaking into your days to come all the way along here three times a week.

Please try to make it a real rest not working off the arrears of things but just relaxing. I will be with you, but not obtrusively as a disturbance. I realise that it's been as trying a time for you (nervously) as it's been for me physically and that you've played up wonderfully — as you would, being you. With all my love and blessings now and always.

Tommy

In memory of her love for Tommy, Clare wrote:

Instead of a winding sheet, my love,
I made me a bridal gown.
The tears that fall on your sealed lids
are stars in our bridal crown.

In life, between your spirit and mine
Hovered the mists of pain.
Death hath rent them. Now in the sun
We know each other again.

We run to each other, and clasp and kiss,
And we who were two, are one.
O beautiful Death, who sets us free
From shadows into the sun!

Travel your road. I wave my hand,
My heart rings out as a bell.
You wave your hand. Clear is your voice
Calling a blithe farewell.

Clare and Tommy had spent twenty-seven years together. They were years which had brought many changes; two world wars; good times and difficult times; sometimes they were in funds, sometimes not; sometimes they experienced togetherness and at other times disagreements. They were years of change during which Clare's search for depth and meaning of life had considerably deepened and which also established her as a writer and poet of distinction.

Her involvement with Buddhism continued to have a deep effect on her:

The truths of Buddhism have been an outstanding influence in my life. Applied to the everyday life in the world, they do lead to an ever-increasing liberation, a greater awareness, a fuller understanding of human nature, beginning with one's own, and a growing sense of peace which no outward disturbance can affect for long.

As a humble student of the Dhamma I have not gone very far, having no opportunity to read the Scriptures thoroughly or even to meditate as one is taught to do. Nevertheless, there are those who have mentally grasped the profound psychology of the Abhidhamma and can talk and write in learned terms, yet whose lives are still troubled and chaotic because of the failure to realise, and practise, the fundamental tenets of the Teaching. Without this foundation we are as cowherds counting another man's cattle.

What is it that first attracts us to Buddhism? Dismissing the glamour of a "foreign religion" and a promise of escape from the wheel of birth and death, often we find ourselves carrying on where we left off in some former Buddhist life. This is why we feel "at home" when first introduced to it. But perhaps the primary and main reason for this attraction is the fact of suffering. Until we have suffered deeply, and known the anguish of seeing others suffer, we are not likely to enquire into the cause of suffering. Until we realise the cause, we will not realise the cure, which *has* been found and pointed out by the Buddha.

One of the first things I appreciated in Buddhism, following the acceptance of the Four Noble Truths and the Three Signs of Being, was the necessity for non-attachment. While we are identified with our desires, the fruit of ignorance, how can we hope to understand their origin, or see them for the phantasmal illusions they are? Further, this understanding leads to an ever-increasing compassion, as one perceives men and women everywhere confined in their self-imposed chains of hope and fear, and still believing that the possession of this or that, or having this or that removed from them, will bring them happiness or peace. They fail to see the cause of all unhappiness is mind-made. They fail to see that greed and craving and their multiple progeny have made the world what it is to-day. I think it is not possible to bring constructive material reform by material means unless it is the result of enlightenment, whereby man has wisdom to see and help to eliminate the cause of all wrong states of consciousness.

Hence it is no cause for wonder that many thoughtful people in the West are discovering that the truth of Buddhism can be applied, not only individually but collectively. They see that the practice of Ahimsa will ultimately stem the tides of violence; that the brotherhood of man and every living thing is a fact, so that in harming another we harm ourselves; that the short view of this one life, together with judging by appearances, is the result of ignorance from which all so-called "evil" comes and will continue to come, until the eyes are opened upon the truth.

Yet the Buddhist does not proselytise. It would be useless anyway, until a man's own intelligence is turned upon his inner strife and despair. Yet when he meets a real Buddhist, he is greatly affected by his serenity, compassion, understanding and aura of peace. We can achieve more in our influence upon others by what we are, the state of consciousness we are in, than by articles we may write or talks we may give upon the Doctrine. Indeed, unless these are illumined by realisation, they will be sterile, and lacking in authority, and the sensitive reader or listener will feel this.

So always we come back to ourselves, even though there is no "self", but only a vacuum in which pure Consciousness itself in its various aspects may operate. Unfortunately, in almost all of us that Pure Consciousness is interwoven with and obscured by our present personalities, created by our reactions in past lives, a sum total of effects.

This is where the teaching of Buddhism is so different from other "religions", some of which stop short at a moral code, at ethics, at the modification or transformation of this present "self" in order that it may find bliss in "higher realms". True, the inner truths are contained in most of them, but they have been so neglected or overlaid by literal interpretation, by theology, institutionalism and priest-craft, that the majority of people remain in ignorance, finding it easier to believe in vicarious salvation or postponement of the ultimate necessity of working upon themselves.

For certainly Buddhism has its ethics in the treading of the Noble Eightfold Path, and in this sense the cultivation of self-reliance. Yet the difference lies in that ultimately there is no "self" to be relied upon, any more than there is a "soul" vaguely functioning somewhere within that self, unless it is the psyche of the psychologists. Through the treading of the Path we come to realise the illusory nature of much that we used to think was real.

Yet the merest glimpse of that Consciousness "in which we move and have our being" is enough to help one relax from all strain; is enough to spur one on to a fuller realisation, though it may take many lives; is enough to awaken within us a new sense of freedom and harmony which is utterly different in its vastness and dynamic quality from any other so-called "peace" that we have experienced.

Is this the treading of the Path? I would not know. I only know that this realisation seems to take charge of one's life, bringing order out of chaos, sense out of non-sense (for it is beyond the senses); with a feeling of direction that transcends the ordinary notions, standards and laws of the world. It seems to change the very nature itself, so that the things we once found desirable no longer attract; resentments and hatred are seen to be stupid, and fall away; patience, fortitude, gentleness and so on do not *appear* to be cultivated virtues, but a natural flowering; and when the resistances which caused conflict are outgrown, everything in life seems to fall into its right place. We proceed through our average day effortlessly, despite the "ups and downs" which are part of the life of the world. Another thing — we no longer want to interfere in the lives and affairs of others, having found that the practice of Loving — kindness, Compassion, Joy and Serenity have a far greater effect, though the results may be delayed or unnoticed. It is not our business, anyway.

The practice of Buddhism is not an easy way to truth, but if truth matters to us more than anything else, it will be our guiding star through all suffering and perils. It may mean a revolution in our lives, changing all our ideas, our livelihood, our whole attitude to life, with many outward repercussions upon our circumstances and our relationships.

At the same time, perhaps it is not sufficiently understood that its practice can bring help, wisdom and release to *anyone*, if they are intelligent and sincere, however unlearned and humble. Indeed perhaps the journey for the intellectual is longer, as he has more burdens of cherished ideas and monkey-mind activities to relinquish. The simple person may be one whose "eyes are only a little covered with dust".

Yet, by whatever road we may have come to the Dhamma, there is thankfulness and joy when we find it is true. From "the house on fire" with craving, which was our former habitation, we turn to our Refuge, and there we abide.

With Tommy gone, Clare changed her life-style, left London and moved to the country where her heart belonged. Earlier in 1942 she formed a friendship with Cuthbert Lambert who first came to know her when she gave an address on Buddhism at Caxton Hall at a conference of all religions organized by Swami Avyakyananda of the Vedanta Society. Cuthbert was at this time living as a community member of the group who then owned Bushy Ley Farm, Elmsett, Ipswich, Suffolk. They had corresponded for a time and during the years 1943-46 Clare had visited the farm occasionally until 1946 when the group at the farm decided to break up. Cuthbert was very

Bushey Ley Farm, 1946

much against this and began casting about for support from people who might put up money to allow him to secure the property and start another community going. Clare responded to Cuthbert's request and when they had raised enough money between them, she joined him there in the autumn of 1946.

Clare continued to edit *The Middle Way* from there and another old friend, Leila Ward, remembers her using a converted chicken-house for this purpose: "There was one cow, one horse to drag the great water cart to the stream, about 10 goats and as many people full of airy notions about country life in sugar beet land where the earth was baked to stone in summer and turned to liquid mud in winter." Through *The Middle Way* they met up with other interested parties who joined them over the next few months. For various reasons the new group never really got together and although they had many visitors (paying guests were the mainstay financially and never stayed long) and a lot of interest was shown by members of the Society, Clare and Cuthbert felt they should ask them all to leave, which they did. They then decided to continue as a partnership and from then on the place was a privately run farm. As

Preparing vegetables, Bushey Ley

well as continuing to take paying guests they also had one or two people suffering from tuberculosis who wanted the opportunity to put nature-cure principles into practice. They were already running things on organic lines and nature-cure seemed to be an extension of the general principle.

Leila Ward remembers a special incident at the farm:

Two people sat on top of a haystack. One was my daughter, Jane aged five, the other, Clare aged 52. They had prepared a hollow up there ready for an interesting chat. Jane scrutinized her companion long and carefully and finally addressed her saying; "You're only a little girl really, aren't you?" I can imagine Clare's mysterious smile in reply.

Amongst the countless glowing compliments she received in her long life I believe this one was specially treasured. I often heard Clare repeat this story.

Those days on the farm were spent in quite primitive conditions. Looking back on them Clare said: 'It was hard work but I was very happy and treasured memories remain of sleeping on a haystack, stars overhead, of the months of snow and of the friends who came.'

John Bond, another friend, remembers oil lamps about the

farmhouse: 'There were plenty of goats and Clare used to take the milk on her bike to the local village shop.'

In 1948 they were joined by another woman who subsequently became Cuthbert's wife; when their daughter was born in 1949, Clare stayed on to help for a few months but by now she was wanting to do other things. Clare had worked hard at cooking and running the house and seemed fulfilled by it for a time. She was still coping with the magazine and journeying to London every now and again in this connection and to visit her parents in East Ham who, by now, were failing in health. By Christmas 1949 she finally left Bushy Ley and returned to London to look after her ageing parents. It was also around this time that she relinquished the editorship of *The Middle Way*. Having studied all the major religions as a young girl she began to find her sole involvement with one rather limiting and it was said of her that she would keep dragging in Christianity. Deep inside she sought further changes and the challenge of exploring other avenues of belief. She was also finding Buddhism too intellectual and after twelve years as editor of *The Middle Way*, Cyril Moore succeeded her.

During the next thirty years Cuthbert Lambert only saw Clare once or twice although they kept in touch, but he recalls that when he last saw her:

> I took the opportunity to tell her then that I felt somewhat guilty that she had put so much work and hope into her stay at Bushy Ley but in the end got very little out of it. To my surprise she told me that it probably represented the happiest time of her life. She regretted none of it.

4

The Winds of Change

There are times in the life of each and everyone of us when 'the winds of change' bloweth, causing us to make decisions and pushing us in a different direction. These are times when readjustments have to be made; new commitments taken on; a duty performed or a further step in faith embarked on. The early 1950s brought such changes for Clare.

Returning to London to look after her parents, Clare needed to make many readjustments:

> I remember during middle age, ever rebellious, caring for my ageing parents in that same little house where I lived at five years old, even though much had happened in between, crying out in resentment; 'But I do not belong here! Why do I have to go on doing this!' Swiftly the answer came: 'Because you abused power in several past lives, and had to be brought low.' It sufficed; there was no more resentment, only profound humility and thankfulness.*

Clare not only believed deeply in reincarnation but had, at different times in her life, experienced glimpses of lives she had lived before: as a gypsy; as a nun; and as a courtesan; she could also recall long-forgotten memories linked with Tibet and ancient Greece. The doctrine of reincarnation was entrenched in the depths of her soul. The belief that we have lived before in some other bodily form was expressed in the writings of Pherecydes and Pythagoras in the sixth century BC, and earlier in the Vedic scriptures. Millions of Buddhists and Hindus have always believed in it and it is also accepted now by many more people in the Western world. The doctrine of reincarnation also forms the substance of *The Tibetan Book Of The Dead* which was very much a signpost in Clare's life. The book confirmed, and was instrumental in awakening, after-

---

* From 'Involvement', first published in *The New Humanity* by courtesy of the editor, Johann Quanier.

63

Clare in the late forties

death experiences and recollections of earlier lives. Clare had also found, along with many others to whom this belief is very real, that certain problems and reasons for suffering, to which there seemingly are no answers, do find a solution and are understood, if reincarnation is accepted.

John Bond further recalls:

Clare left Bushy Ley Farm to return to East Ham to look after her parents as her mother was ill and her father was blind. I met her at Cronley Truth Centre, Ilford, and found we only lived a few hundred yards from each other. We turned the front room of her family home into an office cum sitting room where Clare answered her correspondence. Having relinquished the editorship of *The Middle Way* she bought the magazine *Here and Now* from Derek Neville. From her home Clare pieced the magazine together and we would take the copies which were sent out to the central Post Office in shopping bags. Clare shopped in the mornings for her parents who were not vegetarians like we were. Clare would take her blind father to the local park then come home to cook for them. On cold days Clare would wear her cloak which stood out amongst the local working people. At times we would relax listening to 'Sheep May Safely Graze' on an old portable gramophone.

The family home was old and there were plenty of tasks to be done to keep it in order, including an open fire with an old-fashioned oven which needed daily attendance. In the front room we had a fire-glow oil heater. We loved the sound of the stove working.

We would entertain her friends with afternoon tea, home-made brown bread and cakes which Clare baked once a week. Clare seemed to live in eternity and was so relaxed whenever she was working or walking. A photograph of Tommy was always kept on her desk in the office.

There were times when we would walk for hours in Epping Forest. She loved her 'cuppa', so we made a fire and boiled the water for the Maté tea which she so much enjoyed. In the evenings we would have a cup of dandelion coffee together and then a quiet time before I left to go to my mother's home. Clare took up pastel drawing and her flower drawings in particular had a living life of their own.

We would go on holidays together looking after YHA hostels for Leila Ward who knew Clare well. She would always keep up her correspondence every day even though she was on holiday. She was always doing things for folk with Bio-chemics |(homeopathic tissue salts) or Dr Bach's flower remedies.

Clare enjoyed the simple things of life and saw eternity behind the beauty in everyday affairs. There never seemed to be a rush on anything but there were many things to settle up. Working and experiencing life

Clare picnicking with her sister-in-law

with Clare I really got to know her and her wonderful warmth in everything she did. She often said, "All life is flux" and she lived that way.

Sophy Ropner, Clare's sister-in-law, remembers her playing the piano very well. Sophy and Clare were close friends and when Cliff (Clare's brother) and her mother both died of cancer in 1951 and 1952 respectively they were very supportive to each other in their loss.

On readjusting to life in the city again Clare wrote the following:

THE BACKCLOTH

I live in London, and it is my custom to take a walk round the familiar streets every evening for a little fresh air before bed. Always I look up at the sky, since its serenity at all times, even when clouded over, helps to restore my sense of values. It is always so untroubled, so vast and, I almost said, so happy. My own little troubles or problems become dwarfed, and so perhaps I am able to breathe in more than physical fresh air. When there is an unusually beautiful sunset, I wonder why everyone is not standing and staring at such pageantry. It has been said before I think that if we saw the sky or the stars only once a year, how much more we should appreciate its ever-changing splendour! Yes often I have felt that the Curtain, beautiful as it is in all its colours, has not yet risen, or the play begun. True, in rare and privileged moments we almost seem to hear 'the music of the spheres' behind the scenes, stand on the edge of a mystery about to be revealed, and are aware of what might be termed the tuning-up of some sublime orchestra. Such are inspiring moments, and we long to see and hear more.

Or we may be looking at flowers in a garden, or just a bowl of flowers in a room. If we are very quiet and still, almost they seem to speak to us. What is it they are telling us? The botanist will never know, but the poet may, and the contemplative often does. It has been said that the flowers in their purity are nearest to the Heart of God, and have not suffered the corruption that some of the other elements and kingdoms have. This is why they enchant us so, and perhaps this is why we take flowers to the sick. Though we may not know it, there is great healing in the flowers. Even as there is healing in the countryside for those who are fevered and over-strained by the life of cities. What is it they are telling us, through the backcloth of petals and stamens, of delicate design and colour? Have you ever looked at them through a little botanic glass, for wonder rather than for information? A new world is revealed. You can travel down the trumpet of a lily into infinite vistas of beauty and peace. Yet you are also aware of a more dynamic sense of life than in the world you look at every day with such ignorant and unobservant eyes. It calls you — to awaken, to explore. The flower has called forth your recognition and response, for beauty is in the eye of the gazer. You have entered a new dimension. The backcloth stirs, grows more transparent .... Then someone comes into the garden, or into the room, and the flower seems ordinary again. Yet you have penetrated a little into a new country, upon a wonderful adventure. You feel there is more than meets the eye in the fairy-tales and the imaginations of children.

Or perhaps you are walking through a wood in summer, and it is a windless afternoon so that the leaves are motionless and no birds sing. Yet the silence is a living one, pregnant with unheard sound, vibrating with unseen movement. The trees are like presences, and even the grass seems holy and aware of something that is hidden from you — the intruding mortal. You walk almost on tip-toe, or you sit at the foot of a tree, and listen, and look, and the spirit of the forest comes out to keep you company. You may learn much at such times for which there are no words at all. You return to your normal self and normal routine, and do not tell anyone of what you have been feeling. Not only you cannot, but it is in some way sacred. The backcloth has been lifted a little for you, but as yet the eyes are not sufficiently purified or trained to see, or to understand the play being rehearsed behind the scenes. You have been very close, nevertheless, to one of God's finer kingdoms behind the scenes, which is forever in action, creating, sustaining, adjusting and restoring the outer world that we see with these outer eyes. Unfortunately, man does not co-operate. He exploits the earth (as well as his fellow-man), and its creatures. He cuts down the trees, violates the naturally fertile earth by introducing strange chemicals in the name of progress. As if this were not enough, he experiments with newly discovered forces in the name of science not only for material ends but for violently destructive ones. The warnings of earthquakes, strange minor happenings and vagaries of the weather do not appear to deter him. The backcloth of the beautiful world which *could* become so transparent that it could clearly reveal the Divine, becomes instead more dense, and its originally pure patterns distorted. Only here and there, though in every-increasing numbers, are the spiritual pioneers in all spheres, the dedicated and discerning ones, seeking to restore that pattern, that it may be upon the earth as it is in Heaven. Will the day come when the backcloth of the earth is rent, even as the veil of the Temple? If man will not contemplate and see, is he to have a rude awakening? But I digress a little . . . . Some of us have known those rare and memorable moments when there seemed to be a light over common things 'that never was on sea or land'. We do not know how it happens. It may be the sight of a haystack in the evening sun; a field of ripening grain; swallows in flight; a certain grouping that makes a perfect picture and makes us catch our breath. Or that light can pass over an ordinary plain face and transform it, and the next moment the inner illumination is withdrawn. Yet we have seen . . . . Or something delicate, tender and lovely may come to us through the touch of a hand. Even any ordinary room, any ordinary group of people can be re-informed and hence transformed by something that has entered the atmosphere, so that we see that room, know those people in a new way. Everything comes to life, is harmonious, strangely moving. We have 'seen through' the backcloth. We wonder if Heaven is like that. I believe Heaven *is* like that. 'We see as through a glass darkly, but then face to face . . . .' and 'when that which is perfect is come, then that which is in part shall be done away'. That which is in part shall be done away. That which is not whole. Yet when the eye is single, then the whole body is full of light. If the eye is single in the steadfastness of its gaze upon God, then gradually the whole being is filled with His Light. Those who have the vision see the evidence of, nay, very existence of God — in His handiwork, in the souls of men and women however overlaid and obscured. They touch the Hem of the Garment, which reaches to infinity, and since they recognise it as the Garment of God, they are healed of whatever has troubled them.

This is what happens when, perceiving the hidden beauty in a landscape, hearing some chance phrase, receiving some unexpected kindness, or reading an inspired book, suddenly we are lightened of all our burdens and feel blessed, comforted, made whole. We have touched the Hem of the Garment. Or to return to our subject, the backcloth has become a little more transparent and we have a glimpse of eternity.

I believe the backcloth of the natural world, the outer forms of things, *is* the Hem of the Garment, for there is no place where God is not. Yet how much He needs us, everyone of us, to seek His will so that we may co-operate with Him in cleansing the lowest hem, our world as it has become in this materially-minded age! We say it automatically: 'Thy will be done. Thy kingdom come, on earth as it is in heaven.' It cannot, unless we help to make it so. God cannot use us in this way, or in any way, until we have given ourselves to Him.

First the recognition, and then the cleansed heart and mind, and the transformed life. These are what God asks of us, so that what is true eternally may become true in fact and in time. And the backcloth will become more and more thin, until its purpose has been served, and 'that which is in part shall be done away', and it will be on earth as it is in heaven. The curtain will go up, the sons of the morning shall shout for joy and there shall be a new heaven and a new earth.

Here and Now magazine which Clare bought from Derek Neville in 1950 was devoted to:

Drawing attention to the holiness of all life. To discourage exploitation, whether of people, the earth, or common things. To encourage co-operation instead of competition; to help forward the ultimate brotherhood of man. It has a pacifist attitude, and encourages vegetarianism to offset the exploitation of animals. To encourage a positive attitude in the midst of negation, and hence publishes articles, short stories and poems that are likely to inspire and refresh; stands for simplicity and sanity and the restoration of true and enduring values.

Originally founded by Derek Neville in 1939 who, himself, was a poet and mystic. *Here and Now* stood for many of the values and beliefs which Clare held in the depths of her heart. Using her parents' home as a base for the magazine's activities Clare spent whatever time she could on keeping the magazine in circulation for the next few years.

Ida Bibby who first met Clare in the early 1950s remembers when her friendship with Clare began:

A friend sent to me a copy of *Here and Now*, its refreshing tone pleased me. Later, I posted to its editor, Clare, a short poem 'The Sickle', which was kindly accepted, with the apology that she could only offer five shillings, but she would like to write to me again.

Clare at this time was living with her blind father. The strain of nursing her mother who had recently died, still in her face. In the January of 1952 she came to stay with my little family of four in the country. My husband, sister-in-law and little daughter of five and a half. She was a gentle guest. She brought her typewriter with her, busying herself on her magazine in the mornings. We lived in Staffordshire at that time, and from there we wandered into Derbyshire. A day in Dovedale very specially remembered.

The influence of Christmas Humphries, and his introduction to Buddhism formed much of our correspondence, and seemed to be the measuring of Buddhism against Christianity. First of all I was saddened for I wanted Clare to be all Christian. Later I realised that the two could merge happily, and this to my rather young and narrow life brought its awaking.

I remember a time crossing a field of very small hillocks with its clumps of gorse. Clare was striding ahead, a true daughter of the wild. Momentarily I thought — 'I have not caught up to Clare completely, but I know that she has something that I must follow.'

For a number of Octobers I visited Clare at East Ham. We wandered through Epping Forest together. In the mornings I walked through the park with her father, Charles Wells, a splendid gentleman. I was always impressed by the importance of his white stick as we crossed the road.

Another time I stayed with Clare at the home of her sister-in-law, Sophy, in Pottersbury. A gentle hostess. Clare and I walked, walked and walked again.

I recall lamp-lit evenings with quiet conversation. Visiting Clare was always an oasis in my busy life.

Ida and Clare corresponded through the years — right up to when Clare died. Birthdays, Christmas and important times were always remembered. On Clare's death Ida wrote: 'It is Clare's deep peace that I shall remember; her wide embrace of God's Loving and the sense of her quiet presence is with me still.'

Out of Clare's awakened heart a deeper understanding and greater receptivity to truth, life and beauty continued to unfold. Through a flower, a cloud, the sunlight, the smile on the face of a child or a saint she became more aware of all those intimations of divinity that touch us gently through everyday experiences. Christ and the Buddha and the great sages have spoken of that divine consciousness which lies at the heart of all things and they lived in conscious awareness of the divine presence so that we might find it. Since her early mystical experiences as a child she had looked

A contemporary photograph of Clare enjoying a peaceful garden

through her physical eyes with the vision of the soul, often remembering some state of being that once we knew. Through her writings and poems she has often spoken of that hidden splendour expressed through the handiwork of nature, the arts or through ordinary faces which can light up as if suddenly illumined from within.

In the May 1952 issue of *Here and Now* her editorial beautifully expressed her increasing perception of this inner light:

WITHIN YOU

The Kingdom of Heaven is within you. How few of us really know what it means! We believe it to be true, perhaps through having heard it so often, yet we remain unhappy, weary, sometimes sick and often bewildered, and are conscious of a kingdom of chaos rather than of heaven within us. We search outside for it every time we look for happiness, security, peace of mind, not only materially but in anguished prayers to a God we have made in our own image. He is still somewhere beyond us, as we strive to reach Him.

In the kingdom of apparent chaos of our world to-day attempts are made to adjust and cure effects rather than to reach and understand the causes of our problems — which are in ourselves. Scientific discoveries and social reform take precedence over spiritual principles, and material benefits cover the stark fact of spiritual impoverishment. We are still looking without, and not within. This is not to decry materialism, but to suggest that until it is open to the Kingdom of Heaven (even as the earth to the rays of the sun which brings forth her hidden flowers and fruit), obedient to its laws and in tune with its rhythm, all our efforts individual and collective will ultimately come to nothing.

But first we must have some knowledge of 'heaven', whose nature is perfect order, beauty, purity, love, wisdom, peace. It is not a place, but a state of being; not static but dynamic in its creative flow and power. It is LIFE, running free or blocked according to whatever room we make for it in the bodies, minds and hearts of these little lives of ours.

It created and potentially dwells in every cell of our flesh, as it created and dwells in every flower-petal, scrap of bark, iridescent gem, bird-wing, fish-scale, snowflake, dust and star, in the wind and sun and the rain which falleth alike on the just and the unjust, and in every thought and feeling of the human heart. For without this constantly creating LIFE all life would cease. Yet we, who might be gods, remain pigmies in our understanding and achievements, and while making rather a sorry mess of things, are still blind enough to imagine we can do everything by our own powers, in our own way, in our own time! To misuse LIFE in the ways we do, would be blasphemy if it were not just pitiful ignorance. For by our greed, fear or evasion, we strangle the Power with us, turn simplicity into complexity, shut out the light and warmth of the Sun, and cover the peaceful innocent memories of Eden with our speed, acquisitions, trivial little pre-occupations, frantic searching (lo here, lo there) and the anxieties of the average day. O when will we learn! "Have I been so long with you, and ye have not known Me?"

Have you ever wondered what was the oil in the lamp of the wise virgins of the parable, so that they were ready when the Master came? The word occurs often in the Bible, for anointing as well as illumination. When the oil of love and humility is dried up through pride, resentment, or bitterness, our muscles harden and the bones become rigid. Break a spiritual law and it works right through to the physical body. Also a lamp, however efficient, without oil will not burn. If you consider it, you will find it has something to do with the LIFE which is the health of the body, the illumination of the mind, and the wisdom of the heart.

For all that is of the Kingdom of Heaven is not remote; it is not of 'the hereafter'. It passes through time yet is not of it. It is 'here' as well as 'there', and not 'then' but 'now'. It is not just in God. It is in *you*.

How can it be in you when you are not at peace, and unhappy, sick, poor, or ignorant? Only because you do not know it is within you, and have never learned to recognise or call upon its inexpressible Power, Wisdom, Order, and Beauty, which restores and heals everywhere and everything in which it is allowed expression. Heaven is the natural territory of the soul, but the soul is not a separate organ. She manifests in every place into which she is called, the movement of the limbs, the spontaneous gesture of the heart, the thoughts she is allowed to set free and re-direct.

Recognition can be awakened in us by an ordinary face become suddenly beautiful, transfigured by an inner light; by a landscape that looks almost divine; by some heroic deed which surpasses human endeavour; a miraculous healing; the balm which falls like cool dew upon a sorrow; a rare communion in which we forget ourselves in the union with one we love, when we are briefly released from our separateness and fear.

As I was writing these words, a man called for the rent, just an ordinary man on a bicycle. He had been ill, and at the open door we talked of remedies, our way of life which sets up conflict, the frustrations which are often the cause of illness. He began to tell me of his hobby of painting, and his eyes shone and his face lit up. He spoke of the joy of colour, of sharing it with others. For a few moments he came to LIFE, and so did I. As I shut the door after his departure I felt we had been sharing a bit of 'heaven' and were refreshed. You see, 'although it is closer than breathing, nearer than hands and feet', it is not something visible, tangible (though at times you can see and feel it with inner sight and touch). It is not provable to the intellect although it is not separate from the earth. Yet you cannot capture it, for its nature is absolute freedom. Only when you have let go of all things do you become part of its inexpressible freedom and bliss. Just as ignorance, greed or fear pull a man apart (resulting in so much nervous tension today) so the heavenly power 'pulls him together' in integration after its own image of wholeness and holiness.

Now in the spring-time, the blossom time, come into your green pastures, rest by your still waters, and take your inheritance which has always awaited your awakening from the sleep of life into LIFE.

With her mother and brother gone, Clare's only blood relative was her father. Clare had always felt closer to her father. His warmth and understanding embraced her sensitive and poetic nature. She had always felt more distant from her mother who had always been quite strict and rigid.

Her days were now filled with seeing to the needs of her blind father, running the house, painting, writing for, and maintaining the existence of, *Here and Now*, visits to a concert or the theatre and occasional days spent in the country whenever possible.

It was at this time that Clare became drawn to the teachings of Sri Aurobindo, his integral yoga* which incorporated the three higher

* Yoga — a Sanscrit term meaning union with the Divine.

yogas of the way of action, the way of knowledge and the way of love. *The Times Literary Supplement* described Sri Aurobindo as "the greatest spiritual philosopher of modern India, one who combines in his vision the alacrity of the West with the illumination of the East'. Along with some other friends who also were drawn to the teachings of this great and influential teacher she founded the original Sri Aurobindo Centre in London. A close friend and founder member, Norwenna Donnelly (who wrote *Founding The Life Divine* — The Integral Yoga of Sri Aurobindo) recalls:

> Neither of us had anything to do with the present Sri Aurobindo Society, which was a much later organisation. We started a small informal group with three friends — Margaret Forbes (painter), Doris Tomlison (founder of the Delves House Trust, homes for retired professional people) and Peter Crampton-Chalk, an accountant and close friend of Doris and also of Clare's. It was a completely 'open' group, not official in any way and as far as I can remember we met every month at Queensberry Terrace where Doris was secretary, to talk, have a shared meditation etc., and lunch. It was very pleasant; we were all great friends and sometimes other people would come who were 'Aurobindians'. Arabinda Basu (Spalding Chair Durham University) was one; Dick Batstone and Alan Cohen coming later. There was also a very glamorous French woman who would fly from Paris occasionally, called Diane. She looked exactly like Nefertiti; was plainly very well-heeled but looked upon with some suspicion by the Ashram!
>
> Margaret, Clare and I were always more deeply in sympathy with each other, I suppose because Margaret was a painter and Clare and I writers. We also had, I think, a fundamentally different approach which is difficult to define — perhaps it was more creative and catholic. Both Peter and Doris were business people. They tended to run the meetings like business meetings with someone in the chair, and 'minutes' etc. and I remember this irked Margaret considerably. She was a disciple of the Tibetan (Dhut Khul). Clare was always basically I think a Buddhist. They were both people of wide and deep experience who, though they enormously admired Sri Aurobindo, did not want this admiration to be a limiting factor on further experience and exploration. I was very much younger and though devoted to the teaching, wanted, like them, to widen the group to discuss other teachings and to welcome other points of view. We also felt that it was wrong for anyone in the group to adopt an authoritarian stance and to reverse decisions we had all made together. There was never any question of breach, but gradually the three of us were able to withdraw tactfully.
>
> I went on to learn a great deal from Narada Thera, who founded the Buddhist Vihara in Beaufort Place and sometimes Clare and Margaret

came too. The centre went on and various Indians were gathered in, although Alan left later to return to his Jewish roots.

I cannot remember how long we three continued in the group before our unease began — quite a long time I think, perhaps about two years. Looking back I remember most the deep sense of fellowship I had with both Margaret and Clare.

In later years Clare often remarked to me on how valuable the teachings of Sri Aurobindo had been at that time in her life and on how he had been an essential signpost on her spiritual journey. In an article which she wrote for the *Sri Aurobindo Circle* she expressed how much his teaching meant to her and how she had arrived at it:

In common with many introverts, for as long as I can remember, I have had memories of a Golden Age, though whether they derived from unrecorded history in time or from intimations of eternity I have never known. Born and reared in a city, I was not very happy as a child, for the world appeared drab, as if shrouded in some way, and the people about me, for all their well-meaning kindness, alien. It seemed I was an exile, though knowing not from where, just as I did not know where my kin might be found. It was all very bewildering, and more so because, since one did not know what questions to put, there could be no answers. For when you do not know what it is you have lost, where shall you look for it? And grown-ups look puzzled and concerned and take you to the doctor.... Gradually you grow up. The bells are heard less distinctly in the soul, but you hear their echoes in running brooks, the wind in the trees, in the words of the poets and musical phrases. You find them transfixed in architecture and paint, and fugitive in landscapes and changing skies, and sometimes there is a look in another's eyes so that your heart beats faster. *Now* you begin to know what you are looking for, though you can only call your search for beauty, truth and goodness THAT, the Nameless, the 'Isness' of things. Naturally devoted and inclined to worship, perhaps you discover religion, and here and there the great doors open a little, and in that Light you see, and in that Silence you hear, and in that Love you are embraced. The mystical experience wherein all things are seen to be One, and you never forget. Your wounds are healed, your loneliness comforted, and with renewed courage and hope you go on. But the great doors of insight close, the Light that illuminated all things and made even the folk about you seem god-like and blessed, is again shrouded in the dust of the world. You feel bereft ... until one day you meet someone who feels as you do, who has heard the Singing from the Sun, and who is travelling the same way as you are. O what bliss to meet such a friend! You discover for each other the Lost Lands of legend, the states of being spoken of in the ancient books, and a way is made for your bright feet through the shadows of the world.

By necessity though, the clouds of glory become a little draggled. They lose their lustre in a civilisation that educates you to compete with your fellows, that teaches you how to live more or less decently but seems to have little or no acquaintance with that winged immortal within you; that scarcely teaches you even to think for yourself, or lead you to the power of your creative imagination, whereby you are linked with God; a civilisation that exploits earth and beast and man, whose standards however progressive are almost entirely material, and whose gods are money, speed, acquisition, power and success. Even religion, so-called, is mixed up in it all. And the consequent ills of all these, by the law of cause and effect, are crime, corruption, neurosis and the dry tinder of conflict in individual and nation ready at a touch to smoulder into flame.

By now you will have read a little of the cycles of history in the birth, rise and fall of civilisations since Time began. You shrink from the menaces of every kind implied in the imminent fall of your own. O winged immortal, whither is the way?

Back you go again to the consolation of philosophy, to the seers, the sages, the Way-showers in all ages and tongues, and bathe for a time in that Ineffable Light which transcends all earthly limitation and ignorance, and you find your freedom in the aspects of the truth they revealed. How serene and pure and crystalline the air from those heights! You are refreshed and feel your god-like nature unfolding within you once again, for, in the famous words of Plotinus, you have taken your 'flight from the alone to the Alone'. And for that very reason you have to come back to the market-place, the sick bed, the battlefield, the humdrum life, your fellow man, your very average, ignorant, clumsy and unhappy fellow man. And well that it should be so! (O teach me, bright immortal, the true way).

At length, after considerable suffering, you accept your earthly conditions, your training-ground (since an angel does not come to earth for no purpose) and in all humility endeavour to practice what the Way-showers have taught you in language that is timeless and universal, and which is illuminated by flashing insights. *These* speak to your soul, and you call out in recognition and answer. At the same time they show you what a mess your life is, the chaos of your thoughts, the conflict of your desires and aims, as under a burning glass. . . . So you practise disciplines, but something within you is vaguely ill at ease, not through the inertia of the natural man, but as if you were looking at the branches and not the roots. You are faithful in good works, but somehow they are automatic, as by a super-imposed, instead of an inherent, virtue. You try to love all those about you, enemy as well as friend, but all you can manage is a somewhat tepid benevolence and goodwill, which in your heart you know to be pseudo and sterile. You pray — ah, how you pray! — in supplication and anguish to a god you have made in your own image, projected from your need according to what you suppose to be your fulfilment and consummation. What impertinence! (Teach me how to pray, child of God within me.) You sit in meditation, shutting out all distractions, trying for peace of mind and soul until you grope towards the fact that only in its opposite — total surrender of all that you are and hope to be to the Nameless — are you able to feel the cool touch upon the brow that relaxes body, mind and spirit. That, ultimately, is all you have. The books, the teachers, the ethical codes, your own efforts, fail you. *They do not go far enough.* Neither do they come near enough. There must be some great secret that eludes you, that has always eluded you. How cabined and confined you are in your ignorance!

The senses pull you towards beauty, freedom, love. The spirit (so you have been led to believe) would call you away from them. The tension pulls you asunder. There is an abyss you cannot cross. Then someone, on a summer's day in a garden, lends you a book. It is called *The Synthesis of Yoga* by Sri Aurobindo. You read it all the way home in the train, and far into the night, and every night until the last page. Pencil in hand, you read it again. You live with it. It becomes part of you. Surely this is the bright immortal speaking? Enfolded and uplifted by its sweeping cadences, it takes you again ito the crystalline atmosphere of the spirit. Yet, you have not, as heretofore, left the earth. The divine life, dynamic, embryonic, can be, is, here and now. For "the Divine that we adore is not only a remote extra-cosmic Reality, but half-veiled Manifestation present and near to us here in the universe. Life is the field of a divine manifestation not yet complete; here, in life, on earth, in the body ... we have to unveil the Godhead; here we must make its transcendent greatness, light and sweetness real to our consciousness, here possess and, as far as may be, express it. Life then we must accept in our Yoga in order utterly to transmute it; we are forbidden to shrink from the difficulties that this acceptance may add to our struggle." And "it is not either of these sides separated from the other, but rather a harmony of the inner and outer life made one in fullness and transfigured into a play of something beyond them which will create the form of a perfect living. The conversion of our thought and feeling without a corresponding conversion of the spirit and body of our works would be a maimed achievement."

As you read, there is a noticeable difference between this book and all the others on Yoga which, for all their wisdom and practical help, did not stir you as this book stirs. You feel the unknown Master wrote not *about* Yoga, but *from* the Yoga, in all its fullness, splendour and, most important of all, its possibilities for *you*. Here is no denial of life, but glorious affirmation. Free from the constricting dogmatism of lesser minds, you breathe deeply and freely of the divine air which is native to you, and which instinctively you recognise to bring health such as we have never known. There is also in all its details and subtlety, your suffering, bewilderment, struggle, but also the promise and the goal. Everything falls into place, and makes sense. Someone has been the way before you. Someone has gone on ahead. You know now the nature of the journey. You have a map of the territory. It is no longer dark, and you are no longer alone. "Life is the field of a divine manifestation not yet complete...." Yes, this is what you always felt to be true, contradicting those who flee the world in order to enjoy the bliss of a personal liberation. For 'life is indispensable to the completeness of the creative spiritual realisation, but life released, transformed, uplifted, not the ordinary mentalised human-animal life ... not even the divine and the undivine mixed together. Whatever may be done by other world-shunning or heaven-seeking disciplines, this is the difficult but unavoidable task of the integral Yoga; it cannot afford to leave unsolved the outward works of life, it must find in them their native Divinity...." How often too have you found in the orthodox consolations of religions "a partial irradiation of our action more subjective than objective, modifying existence perhaps, but without force to change it". Whereas the purpose of *this* Yoga is nothing less than to break up the whole formation of our past and present which makes up the ordinary material and mental man and to create a new centre of vision and a new universe of activities in ourselves which shall constitute a divine humanity or a superhuman nature. This will mean that "there must be implanted and activised in all our doings a supreme, impersonal, unfaltering and unstumbling will in *spontaneous and untroubled union with the Will of the Divine*". For should it not indeed be like this, as a flower opens to the sun or a tree expands and grows towards the light? And while there must be a steady consecration and a total concentration to the exclusion of all lesser aims, "this exclusiveness will in the end exclude nothing except the falsehood of our way of seeing the world and our will's ignorance". Vigilance is stressed again and again, for "all interference from below that would falsify the truth of the superior action must first be inhibited or rendered impotent, and it must be done by our own free choice. A continual and always repeated refusal of the impulsions and falsehoods of the lower nature is asked from us and an insistent support to the Truth as it grows in our parts; for the progressive settling into our nature and final perfection of the incoming informing Light, Purity and Power needs our free acceptance of it and our stubborn rejection of all that is contrary to it, inferior or incompatible." Yet (and is this not also our experience?) even in the midst of these rugged necessities "the divine working can manifest from time to time as a promise before it is finally settled and normal to the nature. Always too there is something higher and greater than the individual which leads him even in his personal labour and endeavour. Often he may become, and remain for a time, wholly conscious ... of this greater leading behind the veil...." And what a comfort this is when it is felt to be so, giving fresh courage and ample compensation for the suffering, the efforts so hardly maintained! For now you know why you were never satisfied with half-measures, the modifications of our nature, the ethical codes, the emotionalism that passes for religion, and the pseudo-spirituality of the cults that, in their attempts to break away from orthodoxy, brought their perceptions of the truth down into impure vehicles and distorted them. Now you know why the soul, the inmost being hidden within and felt only in its rare influences, "prefers rather a purifying suffering and sorrow to degrading satisfactions, love winged upward and not tied to the stake of egoistic craving ... beauty restored to its priesthood of interpretation of the Eternal". And while that call is there "no reproach or egoism, no mere outwards summons of altruism or duty or philanthropy or service will deceive or divert it from its sacred longing and its obedience to the attraction of the Divinity within it".

Again and again Sri Aurobindo insists that 'good works' as such are not only sterile but very degrading (as well we know from observation and experience) when produced from ignorance, (in order to give the ego self-expression and enhance its pride), through slavish imitation or as a result of erroneous teaching. For "it is a spiritual essential change of consciousness, not the surface manipulation which is the method of Mind and Reason, that alone can make Life other than it now is and rescue it out of its present distressed and ambiguous figure".

And here was another signpost I had passed, while hesitating at the fog before me. "At best, we are satisfied if we arrived at a modified and disciplined egoism not too shocking to our moral sense, not too brutally offensive to others. And to our partial self-discipline we give various names and forms; we habituate ourselves by practice to the sense of duty, to a firm fidelity to principle, a stoical fortitude, or a religious resignation, a quiet or an ecstatic submission to God's will. But it is not these things that the Gita intends, useful though they are in their place; it aims at something absolute, unmitigated, uncompromising, a turn, an attitude that will change the whole poise of the soul". How well I had known that ecstatic submission to God's will, before seeing it for the subtle imposter it was! Yet with tender understanding the Master could write: "The idea may be and must in the beginning be inadequate; the aspiration may be narrow and imperfect, the faith poorly illumined or even, as not surely founded on the rock of knowledge, fluctuating, uncertain, easily diminished; often it may be extinguished and need to be lit again with difficulty like a torch in a windy pass. But if once there is a resolute self-consecration from deep within, if there is an awakening to the soul's call, these inadequate things can be a sufficient instrument for the divine purpose. Therefore the wise have always been unwilling to limit man's avenues towards God; they would not shut against His entry even the narrowest portal, the lowest and darkest postern, the humblest wicket-gate. Any name, any form, any symbol, any offering has been held to be sufficient if there is the consecration along with it; for the Divine knows himself in the heart of the seeker and accepts the sacrifice." The East has always been more enlightened than the West in its recognition that the search for the Divine takes many forms, and if the motive be pure and the heart ardent, all are sacred in the sight of God. Sri Aurobindo goes further still in that there is room for everyone in yoga, simple and sage, devotee and intellectual, introvert and extrovert, and for every race and creed. For are not all these aspects of our multiple nature, to be offered for the supreme illumination and purified integration?

As I meditated on the outstanding characteristics of this vital text-book for the divine life, several features shone out. We may have been familiar with the renunciation of the fruits of action as taught in the Gita, but never so clearly *why*. Likewise we are familiar with the necessity for surrender as taught by Christ, but not sufficiently instructed in a practical manner as to what it is that is to be laid down, and the effects of the transformation. The way of the Tao has a similar lovely spontaneity, but may appear dangerously near to irresponsibility to the unperceptive. In *The Synthesis of Yoga* there is no loophole for misunderstanding or evasion. Every contingency, every subtle antic of the ego, every aspiration of the human spirit is portrayed and met. Yet more than these, there stands out the fact that it is the whole being that is to be transformed into the divine — anything short of that implies a falling short of the illumined heights of freedom and bliss; and it is the release of this winged immortal which will best serve the world. Until this is so in more and more individuals, we shall grope in the half-light of a partially instructed ignorance — a totally different thing. And wars, exploitation, neurosis, all the evils of our time will continue, though possibly in more subtle disguises. The second outstanding truth is that the very earth, the universe itself, are implied in this transformation. Have not some of us felt the stirring of the emerging spirit of Nature in the leaves, in the rocks, the very air, urgently seeking our help and co-operation? "We begin to perceive too the key to the enigma of Matter, follow the interplay of Mind and Life and Consciousness upon it, discover more and more its instrumental and resultant function and detect ultimately the *last secret of Matter as a form not merely of energy but of involved and arrested or unstably fixed and restricted consciousness.*" What a subject for

meditation is here, what a call to our uprising, taking all life visible and
invisible with us (as indeed we do, inevitably, since all life is one, from
stone to star)!

As we become freed from all egoistic attachments, freed from the
ignorance and the 'sleep' of unconsciousness in which most of us pass
our automatic imprisoned lives, we visualise the purified art forms, the
recovery of a kingly statesmanship, the beauty of a peaceful social life
which *carries forward* the implications and potencies of the Golden Ages
of legend into our own times and beyond, into infinity.

Rise up, O winged immortal, even in the flesh which is also an
expression of the divine, and enter into your heritage. And bring all
sentient things, everyone and everything which has life, with you. The
Chinese say that "a journey of a thousand miles begins with a single
step", but O the vision ahead!

The winged immortal in Clare recognized the deep truths
embodied in Sri Aurobindo's integral yoga. Here was a doctrine
which expressed with great clarity the practical and actual sanctif-
ication of human life by integrating it with the divine spirit. Her
aspiring soul deeply identified with the teachings of this mystic,
saint, seer, poet and scholar and the essence of his doctrine served to
further release her from the knots and complexes of her bondage.

The great men and women whose lives and aspirations inspired
Clare were Epstein the sculptor, Masefield the poet, Krishnamurti,
Isadora Duncan, Pachmann, Duse, Bernhard, Caruso and Ram
Gopal. These, amongst others, were very much stars in her
contemporary sky. She believed deeply that 'any medium will serve
for greatness to shine upon us,| and inspire us to grow likewise in
stature. For we do not know what we have within us to become."

One such 'star' of whom she spoke with fondness and admiration
was Ram Gopal, India's greatest male dancer whom she had seen
dance in London on several occasions. She often remarked that he
had brought the dancing of the East and its philosophy ever closer to
her heart. Around this time Ram Gopal and his company of dancers
performed at the Royal Festival Hall, London. Clare attended one
of these exceptional performances and was overwhelmed by the
grace of his movements,| his Buddha-like face which was often
wrapt in a mystic trance and his dedication and devotion which
seemed aflame with inner spiritual fire.

Since, as a small boy, he dashed from the house in a monsoon
thunderstorm to dance naked in the rain — Ram Gopal's life had

been dedicated to the dance. Born in Bangalore, in the southern Indian state of Mysore, he was attracted at a very early age to the dances for which this part of India is famous. His knowledge of the religious origins of Indian dancing and his unique ability to communicate through his art every shade of human emotion, movement and thought lifted him into a class of his own. He described his art as 'a religion, a passion, a form of rhythmic Yoga'. His humility and respect for God, expressed through his dance, fanned the flames of that spiritual fire in Clare's own heart to such a degree that, at times, she felt consumed in a divine ecstasy. Ram Gopal had also been deeply touched and inspired by the teachings of Sri Aurobindo. With Ram Gopal she danced in the dance-hall of infinity into the reality of his and her own mystical visions.

To this master dancer Clare dedicated the following poem:

INVOCATION
For Ram gopal

The universe presses upon me
In all its multiple beauty, order and power
Moves in me now the wing-beat
Of eagles, angels and the innocence
(O heart-break innocence) of a flower.

The springs of Being, uncovered,
Well up, but I have no voice to cry
The hail of my spirit perceiving
Its origin in the divine, but only —
Like wind in the trees, a sigh.

I am rent with the veil of the temple
As I watch, as I watch the hands
Moving in ancient rhythms, the running feet
On peaks of snow, the tender obeisance
In fields of Spring, on shining strands.

O sweet release! In my passage
From darkness to the awakening I have met
Strong hands, compassionate eyes, infinite love
Of a gentle leading. My earth's fulfilment
Is at hand, though it may not be yet.

5

Many Gates

Clare's deepest longing was for union with the divine. More than anything in the world she sought that 'full and complete meeting' with God. Often through the years she had experienced glimpses and in illumined moments felt a part of that underlying harmony of the divine world which interpenetrates this one. She *knew* deep within her, as did saints, seers, poets, great artists down through the passage of centuries that there are many gates into the infinite kingdom of God. She believed that some approach through sorrow; some enter through joy; some through faith; some through selfless service and some through walking in fields and woods, to name but a few.

Clare was an eager inner traveller who, in her life, had passed through many of these gates and there were more to come. She had often entered this eternal realm through the open book of nature where her thirsty spirit drank the wine of inspiration and peace in one of the outer courts of heaven. Some like herself also enter through the scriptures of great religions or in the inner sanctuary of their own heart and some find it in the dew of intuition which falls in the new morning of their surrender to that ageless wisdom. She sought to enter through the many gates which daily life presents into that unfolding realm that the mystics *know*; by allowing the spirit to take us through any of these gates we are able to touch the eternal. She often said that, although many men and women of vision had gone before and charted the paths," we ourselves must pass through the gates".

She had learnt in her life that often the gate we are seeking may be in a totally different direction from what we expect, or could have managed. She further realized that anything and everything is a gate when we accept it in love and have the courage to pass through.

Some years previously she saw a mention in *John O'London's Weekly*, the literary journal, of the *Science of Thought Review*, founded and edited by Henry Thomas Hamblin. She sent for a copy and, feeling a kinship with its teachings, it was not long before she was contributing articles to it on a regular basis. In the May 1953 issue of the *Science of Thought Review* she wrote:

THE LOVE OF GOD

As I was going to bed one night I found myself spontaneously thanking God for the day now behind me, for the fresh night air, the peace, the relaxation, the warm bed awaiting me. A voice breathed in my ear: 'You are very precious to me, My child.' It filled me with wonder. 'I? *I* am precious to You?' Suddenly I had an overwhelming and personal realisation of the Love of God, never known so really or intimately before. I knew then that truly I was forgiven of many things that had troubled me for a long time, that I was loved and dear. There was a sense of release, of being made new. I felt as a child must feel when after its bath it is tucked up by a loving parent in whom it has absolute trust. A state of innocence and sweetness, purity, perfect confidence, perfect rest, bliss.

In those few moments I saw that it was silly and meaningless, indeed impossible, to hold any bitter or resentful thought about anyone or anything. People are what they are, and do their best. They get hurt and the pain of it impels them instinctively to hurt in their turn. Then they suffer. They do not know they are forgiven, so how can they forgive?

Forgive the circumstances they find themselves in, the illnesses (of outlook as well as of the body) they suffer from, the conflicts that hold them taut and tense so that they project their frustrations and irritations most irrationally upon those nearest to them.

How can we know we are forgiven and loved, as we always have been and always will be, since Love can do no other? How may we win to the perfect peace and joy the realisation of it brings? And having won it, how may we stay in it, so that we may love others more and 'forgive them, they know not what they do'? Forgive ourselves also as in common with the rest of humanity we stumble and make the same mistakes over and over again?

No man by taking thought can add a cubit to his stature. Thought, however intense, will not lift us into the kingdom of heaven. I think it must be a gift of grace, and that we cannot deliberately win it. It is not a prize for effort. It comes without apparent seeking, though indeed the soul may have been seeking for long ages, without our awareness of it. It is there all the time. But we can turn our hearts and lives — like the children that in essence we truly are, conscious of being defenceless — in the direction of God simply and without fear, and in perfect trust. We can thank God for all that we realise already, all that we have, all our opportunities (and how numerous and vast they are!) and so become more and more aware of the Holy Spirit manifesting through all things and all people and circumstances. Indeed it is our shield and buckler, going before us, seeking to express through all that we feel, think and do.

How eager and willing that Love of God is to meet us, and give to us! More wonderfully than we ever could have imagined for ourselves. How stupid we have been to think we could run our lives alone, by our own efforts! Perhaps we used to pray intensely and in anguish that we might have our difficulties removed, so that we might have relief from worry, security, and peace. We prayed for healing, so that we might suffer no more pain of handicaps; for opportunities to serve others (as if they were not with us every moment!), so that we might fulfill the heart's desire. Or we might have asked just to be made whole, to be granted understanding, illumination, wisdom, and so on.

It seems to me now all a little beside the point. Others may not know what they do. We do not know what we ask. These qualities are by-products, results. None of them are separate from one another. They are all found when we allow God to find us, and to pour His Own Nature through us. Even in our limited human experience, everyone knows that when we love anyone we want to share all we have and are with them. Sharing *is* love, however clumsily in our ignorance we may do it.

How much more so then must be the sharing of the Love of God! We shall feel it, according to our capacity, our readiness to receive it, and our willingness to let it flow through to others *after its own manner*, not necessarily ours.

And *that* is the Love that forgives, that makes all things new, that brings peace, joy, light, a transfigured vision, the ability to go forth into the world fearlessly, a happy, harmonious and full life, all that the soul needs for its joyful experience of eternity here and now. If some seem to be missing (such as when we long to be this or that and seem unable) then there is still a part of us somewhere that is blocked, resistant, fearful. Yet we need not fear. Even if the resistance, the pride, or whatever it is brings suffering, even so that Love will help us to relax (if we let it) and reveal an infinite tenderness.

If then God is Love, then in Love we move and have our being. I am quite sure this is true, as true as the sun is in the sky, pouring its rays down and upon and through every living thing. If only we could *know* it to be true, through all the varied hours, light and dark, of our average day! Others know it, and their lives are testimonies to the support, guidance, power and blessing it brings. And so can we.

On 29 July 1956 Clare's father died of pneumonia at the age of eighty-four. The strain of the last few years had left its toll. Her health had broken down and because of lack of finances she withdrew from circulating her magazine. Her readers were sorry to see the end of *Here and Now* but, in the unfolding pattern of her life, a change of design was in the making. Another one of those gates was in the process of opening through which she was to enter a different territory in which she would be given the opportunity to offer herself in greater service to God. After sorting out the family possessions, she sold-up and rented a flat on Hermon Hill, Wanstead, east London.

From her new place of residence she continued to contribute articles to the *Science of Thought Review*. Her friendship deepened with the editor, Henry Thomas Hamblin, or HTH as he was affectionately known, was an English mystic who had the rare gift of being able to express the deepest truths in a language that is easily understood by all. Clare felt very much in tune with the aims of this monthly magazine which was (and still is) devoted to the teaching of 'applied right thinking'.

Henry Thomas Hamblin and his wife
on the steps of Bosham House

In the words of Henry Thomas Hamblin:

What is termed *Science of Thought* teaches right thinking, i.e. thinking in harmony with Truth. It is the intention of life that we should be happy, joyous, healthy and truly prosperous and successful. By this is not meant worldly success through a ruthless disregard of other people, but a life filled with blessing and harmony, order and the highest good. For instance, there are things so precious that no wealth can buy them. Happiness, peace, harmony, joy, beauty, order, love — these become ours, and also greatly improved health, but no wealth can purchase them; they come as a result of living and thinking in harmony with the laws of our pure being.

Clare and HTH corresponded regularly. On 3rd February 1957 Clare wrote:

Dear Henry,

It is a long time since I sent you an article, for I have been obliged to be quiet for a time, as the new adjustments are made in my life.

So often you are in my thoughts. When the weather is better I would love to come and see you again and sit in silence with you. Meanwhile, God bless you and your work now more needed and helpful than ever to countless numbers of people.

> With my love to you always,
> Clare Cameron

In another letter a few weeks later Clare asked:

I wonder how many you have met, dear Henry, who have a glimmering of the reality of 'the Nothing Between', the surrender implied in the following little couplet by Dr Suzuki (teacher of Zen Buddhism):

> "Wordiness and intellection —
> The more with them the further astray we go;
> Away therefore with wordiness and intellection,
> And there is no place that we cannot pass freely.
> Try not to seek after the true,
> Only cease to cherish opinions...."

For even 'seeking after the true' in spiritual things can be a fetter. The Buddha says that craving for enlightenment even, was still craving. For it is subtly linked with creating God in our own image.

That is why that first of all *you* have helped more than anyone I have met, or read. Secondly, Krishnamurti, who must be one of the very few in the world today who knows something of the underlying reality, the Divine Ground of the mystics, and how *everything* must be surrendered before we can be aware of it. And then there is utter solitude, utter emptiness and loneliness ... yet it is the Fullness of the Void, 'the inmost centre in us all where truth abides in fullness'. Yet very few can stomach Krishnamurti, for he strips us of everything. When I had the privilege of meeting him, I said he taught the inmost core of Buddhism — he replied he had read very few books.

Zen of course points to the same truth. Are you not sad at times that so few can see what is under their noses, as dear old Lao-tze knew so well?

One day, it is all this I want to suggest with my own pen, if it is at all possible.

I remember somewhere in the Buddhist Scriptures we are reminded that the space of the door-frame is what is important; what the jar contains, and not the jar; just as silence between sounds holds the mystery.

... Do please forgive so long a letter. I know of no-one else I can share these thoughts with.

Your friend,
Clare

Krishnamurti, an enlightened seer from the East, whom Clare mentions in this letter, certainly had a deep effect on her. His realizations of truth and guidelines on understanding our nature through an unconditioned mind free of dogma, belief, tradition and conceptualization spoke to Clare's leanings towards learning with an uncluttered and open mind. His instructions on mindfulness, being aware of what is happening in the present moment, confirmed her own experiences and realizations on being ever wakeful and trusting in her vision of freedom.

But it was from Henry Thomas Hamblin that she received the most help. In these times when her life had been more than usually bewildering and difficult his saying: 'A Divine Adjustment is being made in all my affairs, according to Infinite Wisdom and Love,' had brought her through. To Clare, this realization became a mantra when repeated often, each word was like a signpost or winged messenger. She had found that, by dwelling on the *Divine* adjustment, which may not be according to our worldly notions and equally dwelling on *Infinite* Wisdom and Love lifted her into an all-embracing realization beyond her everyday understanding. In taking this Truth as her refuge and obeying what came to her as guidance from within, then the outer life took on the pattern of the inner harmony.

Henry Thomas Hamblin was known widely as a practical mystic. His teachings meant much to Clare and many others because they could easily be applied when facing the difficulties of everyday life.

Clare was always in search for something she had lost. She had found it as a teenager within the pages of *Gitanjali* by Rabindranath Tagore — the discovery of the soul; the restoration of that inner communication with the source of life, the eternal, conscious union with God. Her soul, like Tagore's, cried out for truth, this love of

God; the beloved of every heart. She had studied *The Bhagawad Gita*, the religious classic and scripture of the Hindu religion, books on the teaching of the Buddha and, when she came across the *Tao Te Ching*, the ancient Chinese classic by Lao Tzu, she *knew* she had read it before in an earlier incarnation. This ancient Chinese philosophy was very familiar to her. She had also read the books of philosophers, saints and mystics of the West and often related to these as maps and charts depicting the way to the beautiful country, the divine ground, the kingdom of God.

Henry Thomas Hamblin particularly shared her love of the *Tao Te Ching*. *Tao* means way, path, method; *Te* means power, virtue, strength, righteousness; *Ching* means book. In this unique classic, which has been more frequently translated than any other work except the Bible, the essence of Taoism is contained — the spiritual level of being.

Friends who understood the secret language of such illumined souls who had gone before, gravitated to her and she to them. They shared different experiences: the recovery of ancient memories; their realizations and the books they found helpful. They were all travellers on a journey of exploration and discovery of who and what we are — the spiritual quest — the discovery that the truth, the kingdom of God is within ourselves, right where we are.

In the October 1957 issue of the *Science of Thought Review* she wrote:

THE RIGHT PLACE TO BEGIN

"It's easy, once you find the right place to begin," he said with a smile as he went down the stairs and out into the street. I was left gazing at the imaginative trifle he had made with a few short lengths of wire, a touch of varied and delicate paint, three wooden beads, and a flat piece of planed wood for a base. It was an extremely light and airy impression of a parakeet, and it swayed in the breeze as it stood on the white chest in the hall. It was like something out of fairyland, and he had made it for fun, in half an hour of relaxation.

Over my head swung another of these 'mobiles', one of the latest expressions of modern and experimental art, a little baffling to those used to the familiar forms. This was made of scraps of tin, shaped and curved like waves or petals, suspended also from odd lengths of wire, curved over one another, and held to the chandelier by another long curve of wire. This silvery contraption also moved in the gentlest breath of air, yet none of the petals ever touched one another. It was charming, and yet in some way satisfying, as it expressed a natural rhythm, and held some secret. "It is easy, once you know the right place to begin!"

The right place to begin. A secret known to the wise but which has eluded the clumsy and ignorant since history began, wherein man has struggled with his hands, his inventions, thoughts, feelings, longings and aspirations to shape his private and public world nearer to the heart's desire — and failed so often. A Chinese sage said very long ago: "When we return to the root, we gain the meaning." Another great sage had said: "Consider the lilies, how they grow. ..." My friend of the 20th century, an ordinary fellow, but uncluttered up with philosophical thought or intellectual speculation, had stumbled on the same secret. It was, and is, as simple as that. The charming trifle before me spoke as nothing in a book might do for it seemed alive, part of a natural rhythm, even as the lilies of the field, even though created by the hands of man.

Natural rhythm. Hope sprung up in me swift and strong. Suddenly I saw what Man might do, when he is ready to be enlightened and return to the roots of simplicity and innocence; when he is ready to leave the husks of materialism, competitiveness, ambition, exploitation — all the fruits of greed, fear and ignorance — and turn his face once more to his Father's Home, the simplicity of the Kingdom within his own breast.

"It is easy, when you know the right place to begin ..." Too easy. Since man fell into duality, multiplicity and complexity, he cannot imagine himself achieving anything whatsoever unless it is very difficult. Of course it is difficult, but only because there is so much to be unwrapped, uncovered, disentangled before we may 'return to the root and find the meaning'. It is man's complexity and self-effort that makes it so. Another faculty has to be rediscovered and awakened within him, which some of us call the soul, some rebirth, some transformation, some the Law of Reversed Effort, or Action in Inaction, or Christ in you, and others The Perfect Way, and so on. The terminology depending on the religious creed or the personal approach, does not matter. They all mean the same thing.

They all point the same way, to relaxation and surrender, through the narrow gate which leads to eternal life, which paradoxically is also a broad highway peopled by the enlightened of the ages. The merest glimpse of that eternal life only comes when we are near to it. Books may help us, teachers may inspire us, but they are only signposts, necessary as these are. We ourselves must make the effort.

Yet why this talk of effort when "it is easy when you know the right place to begin?" Because it does require effort of understanding, faith, endurance, steadfastness, courage, serenity and love of God and heavenly things, to be prepared to drop *all* burdens that are hindrances upon the way to ultimate Simplicity and Innocence. We appear to face a Void, and only when we have dared to take it, do we know the Fullness of it, and how it meets every possible need far more profoundly and wholly than we could ever arrange ourselves.

So we have to be born again, and pass through the narrow gate of rebirth, and only those who in our own day feel wedged in that tight and narrow aperture know the preceding anguish, caused sometimes by the resistance to the Divine processes. It is not easy to drop long-cherished ideas, habits, intentions, plans, and all we have hitherto been. We have to cease trying to do anything in our own strength and powers, since that way suffering lies, and always will. Only when they fail us utterly do we approach wisdom and understanding. An old proverb says: 'Truth lies at the bottom of a well.'

Yes. Sometimes, and indeed almost always, we have to be brought very low before we can be raised up. Not without significance our fairy stories, if such they be, of the treasure hidden in the cavern, and the dragons that barred the way before it could be found. Yet only when we are brave enough to go on, alone, apparently helpless, trusting God only, does the miracle happen. While we cling to the shore with a finger we shall never know the mysterious currents of the Stream which carry us in the right direction, because it is in conformity with the natural rhythm of things. While we continue to lay down conditions, we shall never know the perfect freedom which is in 'His Service'. Blind as we are, we never really see until we let God look through our eyes. How supremely logical it is! Only the whole of us can be made Whole, and it is the complete surrender which enables any one of us to move forward as a whole person, at peace with himself.

Have we not found it so? Does not Life, the great teacher, send us back again and again in our tracks to pick up something we forgot about — the evaded responsibility of last month or last year or several years ago, the problem we postponed facing and dealing with, the hidden cowardices or resentments which led us into such unhappy situations and circumstances at the time? This is why, even when our Way is clear through a new understanding, and becomes joyful and significant, we are sent back to gather these odds and ends of ourselves and offer these, too, to God, that He may adjust and harmonize them. They are not failures, and there is no cause for regret. Through going back to them with our new understanding, and a glad readiness to co-operate instead of opposing them as hitherto, they are transformed. Thus we learn the mysterious activity of the Holy Spirit. We all take these stepping-stones of our dead selves, if we will, at one time or another. Is not the forest tree nourished through its roots, as they feed on the withered leaves of yesteryear? They are our foundation for our new life. We call it the maturity of experience.

So let the leaves fall to earth! Cease to cling to what is outworn, while being grateful for their purpose at the time! And as we learn to 'cease to cherish opinions' we find also that 'the Perfect Way knows no difficulties'. We know, too, that 'except a grain of wheat fall into the ground and die, it abideth alone'.

There is the simplicity of it, the beauty and wonder of it. But no, the instinct towards self-preservation, in all its subtle forms, is strong in us. When will we grow up and out of these appearances into a purer sphere where we may come and go freely in the infinity of the True Reality? From where all true beauty, inspiration, joy and power derive? And learn to function there, in that realm where Love is everywhere, and so radiate its atmosphere that others will begin to wonder, and also strive to awaken from the sleep of ignorance that has bound them for so long?

As I thought of the efforts being made all over the world to bring increased understanding so that the nations may live in peace together, I looked up at the silvery mobile above my head, where the petals still gently moved in the light breeze. Not one touched its fellow. Not one hit against the other. There was beautiful and harmonious movement. It was like a ballet, and a mirror of divine goodwill. Need the analogy be pressed? Is not the right relationship in all its aspects the problem and yet the key, to our times? We are being led to cultivate right relationship to the members of our family, our friends (and our enemies, so called!), our livelihood, environment, the objects we use every day, and ourselves. Where do we even begin to consider such a major adjustment?

It is easy, when you know the right place to begin; just as key and lock must be as one before they work harmoniously as one. The right place may lie a long way in, a long way down or a long way up, for in God's sight it is all the same. It seems far only because we have not explored it. It is also very near, for the flash of insight can happen any time, when we give the right response to all experience. When we are one with the natural rhythms.

Sounds difficult. Is it? I looked again at the airy model of the parakeet, shining in the sunshine. My friend had said, 'I made it for fun.' Perhaps there is a clue here. Surely we have noticed the joy that transfigures certain faces, the gaiety of some renowned person playing with a child or a kitten? The truly great are always simple, having dropped the petty clutter *we* carry around with us. Surely we have noticed the ease and serenity some people bring to problems and tasks that would appal us. The busiest folk always have time to stare, and laugh.

You see, 'up there' or 'in there', deep within us, is a realm where everything *is* joyful, light, happy, effortless; where the Light is so clear that the right thing to do is known at once; where a Power works through us, the human instruments and channels, if we do but let it. And we are needed so much, if the Kingdom of God is to transform the earth into Its own image. The One we profess to follow said that His Yoke was easy and His Burden was light. We do not understand this, and only will when His experience is also ours.

When our hands are quite empty, and lifted in all humility to serve in God's Way and not our own, then through the mystery of Grace they are filled with eternal treasure. It will be shared by all humanity, through us. This is the right place to begin, and all the rest will follow. This is where the key fits into the lock, perfectly. This is where the door of time opens upon eternity. This is the source of creation, wisdom, peace, joy and love, and now we are part of it. And only now are we wise and simple enough to show others the right place to begin, and to support them as they seek, since the arrival and release is sure.

Through her awakened consciousness, Clare *knew* of that eternal realm, the entry to which is only gained by an inward process. It is in our own hearts where the truth dwells. Unless we enter into the knowledge of this inner realm we are unable to understand ourselves, others, or the world about us. Her articles, poems, her beliefs continued to provide evidence of this underlying reality.

In inspired moments, nurtured by the beauty of nature, she continued to write verses. About this time the following emerged:

THE DEEP CENTRE

We are as little children
In the vast cradle woven of the stars
That swings to the same rhythm
That moves to the tides and opes the daisy's eye,
Unfurls the leaf of Spring and calls the winds
From the four quarters in their seasons.

Now, in this Deep Heart where all are one,
This faithful beat, support and strength divine,
Flowing in the blood as through all space,
In peace above all passion, purged of pain,
In light and freedom come from starry space,
Take my hand, and look into my eyes.

As the tide upon the shore, wind in trees,
Song in bird-throat, flower upon the stem,
Past the need of loving we are one
Merged in the great rhythms that await
Those who climb the ancient secret way

That leads into God's Heart, the ring of stars,
The ring and swing and cradle of the stars.

NIGHT-PIECE

O Mother, Night, who releases us
From swaddling clothes of day
Wherein we fret, complain and pray,
Into the vaster, sweeter airs,
That quench the cravings, please and prayers
With wind, or dew, or the blessed rain
I seek your wisdom, strength, again.

Majesty, that raises us
Unto stature, breadth and height,
Whose starry gown reveals the Light
Of that Dazzling Dark, once writ
By the seer who visioned it,
In you my freedom streams and sings
Released upon your tireless wings.

Divinity, in whose womb
Everything is given birth,
Galaxies, and suns, this earth,
And all that moves, lives and dies —
So marvellously deep your eyes!
Bent upon this godling now
With the kiss of mountain snow.
Transcending my mortality
I enter your eternity
To become, from depth to height,
Your calm, your peace, your clear insight

O Mother, Night.

In the summer of 1958, Clare left London and rented a cottage with her sister-in-law in Ashdown Forest. She was overjoyed and deeply grateful to move into the country where she felt so much at home. The cottage, at Fairwarp, Uckfield, Sussex was situated on a secluded slope on the top of Ashdown Forest, with a view of the South Downs. The garden of an acre contained many fruit and other trees and a cart track wound down from the cottage to a stream:

Oh the bliss of the country air again, the evenings from the height of 500 feet looking across the valley's glimmering under the evening star, the simplicity, the remoteness. Money was short, for I only had payment for my articles in the *Science of Thought Review*, but I was happy.*

In the September 1958 issue of the *Review* there appeared a fine contribution by Clare:

BEAUTY AND THE BEAST

Often when in trouble, or faced with some dreaded experience, many of us have found comfort in the 23rd Psalm, and cried with the Psalmist: "Yea, though I walk through the valley of the shadow of death, I will fear no evil, for Thou art with me..." This article is an inquiry as to just how the Lord really is with us.

I asked myself why we should fear the 'evil' in the valley of the shadow so much that we ran to the Lord for refuge, as if we were setting the painful and dreaded experience over against the heavenly protection, turning our backs on it, so to speak, so that we might relax in the comfort of the Presence. (You may not do this, but many of us do.) Why was the evil so fearsome, even if we did know it was but in our minds?

Despite the Open Way of Acceptance, the true way into and through all experience, to which our Editor, Henry Thomas Hamblin, drew attention in a recent Editorial (July 1958) and which I found so wise and true over a period of years, still there seemed something instinctive in our human nature that recoiled from the painful and unpleasant, so that we fled to *our own ideas* of the Lord to take us through.

For who and where was the Lord? Did He come from afar at our anguished cry to take us through the valley? That could not be, except in our time-and-place conditioned minds, for the Lord is everywhere, and there is no place where He is not. If that was so, then was He already in the midst of the thing that caused our fear and dread? Then surely His Light and Love and Power were already active, right there, just where we stood, but impotent until we knocked at, passed through, the door of the 'imprisoned splendour'. You see the difference between running away from the human experience into the heavenly one, and realising that actually they are one and the same. One should meditate on this.

It has been said so often by the saints and mystics, the enlightened ones of all ages, that from the higher and wider consciousness of another dimension, from the sphere of the divine wherein we 'see', that there is neither good nor evil as we know it, but only the One in polarity, where all things are seen to be harmonious and most beautifully related in unity. It is we who, in our ignorance, distort the harmony, and fail in

*From the introduction to the 1979 edition of *Rustle of Spring*, Skilton & Shaw, London.

our relationship both to our fellow men and to God because we want this and not that; prefer to go our own way and not in faith as we are led, often through those very experiences which lead us to the promised land of revelation that we can reach in no other way. Our way is the partial way of choice, wanting everything made plain and visible to eyes that have not yet learned to see, so that we may feel safe and secure. God;'s Way is hid in mystery, and it must be so, since our own divinity is also hid in mystery from us. Yet that divinity is everywhere there is life, not in the part but in the whole. We are whole in the measure that we give ourselves to the whole, unquestionably, in perfect faith.

Yet, such is the nature of those temporal and spatial minds of ours, it seemed that we are still looking for the good within the suffering, as if they were two separate things. Then it was natural to recoil from the one and seek the other, and rightly so, since so much of our suffering is brought on by our own ignorance and self-will in all its subtle disguises. And also, it was a half-truth, for the good *was* in the pain, but not in the way our minds tend to imagine. It seemed that it could not become *redemptive and creative* suffering until we abandoned and renounced all our ideas whatsoever! And our cravings and desires too, even for spiritual achievement, attainment, freedom, truth, enlightenment, and all the other words we use to express the soul's sincere longings, even as 'the hart pants for the water-brooks'. These too, Lord? It seemed so.

But why? I wondered if we were to learn to trust our immortal souls more, the divine spark within us, for even on what we feel to be the highest levels, 'he who seeks to save his life, shall lose it'; i.e., all that is ignorant and delusive in us, and of which our bonds are made, and to which in our folly and ignorance we cling for safety. The soul needs to be free of them before it may expand and awaken in the promised land of the illumined consciousness. And all our own ideas were fetters upon the soul's freedom.

Ah, then, the difference! Pain and suffering, like happiness and joy, love and hate, peace and strife, words whose use has such association and connotation that we were imprisoned in those very special associations, which had very deep roots in the racial as well as the personal memory. We had not the least idea of the Reality beyond them. We never would unless we put aside, so far as we are able, all they had come to stand for. Words, like the senses, were gates to be passed through. We were still standing at the gates. We had to pass through to the unfamiliar and the unknown.

And lo, when we ceased to make choices, lay down conditions, aware of the deception of appearances, and were glad and ready not only to accept but to live in and through every experience to the full, there was not only the astonishing relief and joy of release and freedom from fear and all that hitherto bound us, but we found ourselves in an entirely new world. Actually it was the same world, but now we were feeling it from within, instead as hitherto looking at it timorously from the outside. We knew ourselves to be part of Creation itself. The tides of day and night, winter and spring, systole and diastole, peace and conflict, angel and man, flowed through us. It was all part of the Creative Stream, and how sweetly it carried us, and how much more harmonious then life was seen to be, bringing the healing and adjustment of relationship not only of our fellows but to all living things, and the same healing to the tortured heart and tensed body. Having passed through the gates of those very words that had made us so afraid, the gates of memory and dread, we found we were close to the Kingdom of God. An astounding discovery.

You remember how in the fairy tale that Beauty did not run away seeking protection from the Beast, coarse and ugly though he was. She was without fear of him because her love and compassion overcame that fear and dissolved it. She did not love the Prince in disguise because at first she did not know there was a Prince. Quite simply, she accepted him, a fact of experience needing the key of her love to release its inherent reality. Only then did his disguise fall away.

And so with us. There is nothing to be afraid of in the Valley of the Shadow because not only is God with us there, but He is as much the valley as the height. And in order to awaken into spiritual under-standing, paradoxically we often find it in the depths as well as upon the mounts of vision. For God is everywhere, for He is the Fount of Life and Life itself in all its potency and potentiality.

Spiritually speaking, therefore, experience often proves that no amount of supplication eases the tensions of our anxieties or removes our fears, but only the profound recognition *that depth and height are the same*, and they are both of God, and often we are sent down into those depths to find Him. Then indeed we are under the shadow of His wings, wherever we are, whatever we may be passing through, and there is nothing in the whole universe that can make us afraid any more, as our Editor has so well said. We have proved it. The Stream flows on, and we go with it, in all its rhythms and interchange which make the whole — light and darkness, outgoing and withdrawal, sound and silence, suffer-ing and joy, peace and conflict, allowing them to flow through us as they will.

Conflicts, depressions, suffering we may continue to experience, but we shall not fight them any more because they are 'wrong', but seeing them from the deeper reality behind appearances know them as the warp and weft of existence, accept them in that joy and peace which comes from a greater understanding, using them constantly as creative oppor-tunities. How can anything become creative in us while we are fighting or resisting it? And there is no need anyway, for 'the way of the spirit is harmony and peace'. Thus do we begin to apprehend the mysterious

wisdom of God; come to life in a new way in His service, and feel the
healing touch of that peace which is not absent of strife as we know it in
the ordinary way, but lies at the heart of it, where it 'passes all
understanding'.

Through using the difficulties and struggles in her personal life, as
creative opportunities, Clare had found and continued to find peace
and blessing which lie at the depths of such an approach. She had
come to know that those times of darkness and struggle hold in their
grasp the key which unlocks the door to deeper understanding and a
greater freedom. Those times of darkness provide the compost to
nurture the growth of the aspiring soul.

On 28 October 1958 Henry Thomas Hamblin died, an event
which, little known to Clare at the time, would greatly change the
direction of her life. On attending his funeral she wrote:

I shall remember All Saints' Day 1958 as one of the happiest and most
beautiful of my life, where one of the company of saints was laid to rest
in Sussex earth. Those of us who were privileged to be present at the
simple ceremony will always remember the sunshine over the grass, the
peace in the little church by the creek (one of the oldest in the country),
and how we were all caught up in the atmosphere so natural, so serene
and happy that it completely defies description. The prevailing harmony which the theme of his life and teaching so pervaded us that
perhaps some of us will never be quite the same again, as if transported in
that hour to where he had been translated. Though indeed all through
his last illness there had been the awareness of Divine Upholding, and
we knew all was 'well, a thousand times well' as he so often wrote. This
applied to his life-long service as well as the man himself, for were they
not one? We felt that this service was not terminated by any means, but
uplifted and extended both here in the world as well as 'there' over the
Border, and again there was the sense of unity, oneness, between them.
This awareness was so strong that we know that his work will now be
carried forward with a new freshness and vigour by his son, Bert
Hamblin, whom this dear English saint so wisely appointed, and who is
'under direction' from on high. Is there any finer qualification?

As we stood under the trees that serene and beautiful afternoon, one
amongst us said: 'It is like a spring day.' And it was as if he who had
passed on was already in the eternal spring-time, and the work which
was part of him was already on the threshold of a new spring also. Could
it be otherwise, with one to whom the divine realm and the world we see
were one and the same?

An hour before the ceremony I had walked by Chichester Cathedral,
where the four-square tower soared to the blue sky. This too, in its

stability, its ruggedness almost, reminded me of him. In his firmness he was like a rock, so surely based in the Truth that it was as natural as breathing to him to share it with others. Indeed he was a citadel to thousands through the years all over the world. In common with all the great men, he was simple, modest and unassuming always, and by these qualities we recognise the true saint, together with always having time in his exceptionally busy life not only for every visitor (and they were innumerable) but the poor and needy. On that afternoon of his interment, a row of shillings was laid along the doorstep of his home as usual for 'the gentlemen of the road', with a little note promising food on the family's return, so you see how in most practical ways also the good work goes on.

At a time when men and women were failing to find in orthodox teaching the Bread and the Living Water, he was a pioneer who cleared the choked springs for them. Always very clear in his vision, he was alert always to the spurious, the 'fancy' cults, the glamorous and sensational by-paths which lead the beginner astray, and his common sense was outstanding. His eyes were on the stars, for he was of the line of mystics of all ages and creeds, but his feet remained firm in the world which he taught us to see *through* that by our understanding translated into our lives *we* might *bring* through. No one will ever know the number of souls whose lives have become illumined, creative, joyous and serviceable through his books, leaflets, magazine, correspondence courses, and by personal contact. And somehow he found time for all of us. Perhaps he himself knows now that the worn-out vehicle has released him more fully than ever into the Joy of his Lord.

How, then, shall we best remember him? By his wisdom, which was not of time but of eternity? By the Light that flowed to the ends of the earth through him? As the loving, and often humorous friend and father of us all? For he will have kindled a special reaction in each one of us, according to our need.

In the house in the midst of the garden that he loved in Sussex, where he and his wonderful little wife (but great in spiritual stature also, a worthy support and invaluable companion) spent so many years, and in the offices in the garden where his faithful staff work so devotedly, there is an atmosphere that, if it could be repeated in other homes, the world would be a much happier place. Surely that will be the most fitting memorial, one that he would have wished more than anything else, a *living* and *dynamic* testimony of the Truth, the Freedom, the Blessedness of surrender to the Father of us all that he lived and taught? May his work go on ... in our hearts ... for it is boundless and immeasurable.

Soon after his father's death, Bert Hamblin received an offer of help from Clare:

Dear Bert Hamblin,

If I can be of any service to you in your new responsibilities, call on me, though I would have never suggested it except for your remarks after the funeral. It would be a great joy to me to have a talk with you . . .

I feel most strongly that, whatever you may feel yourself in your natural humility and unpreparedness, that this is a divine appointment . . .

To begin with, if you are snowed under with 'problem' letters and have no-one to lend a hand, do shoot them along to me despite my own busy life. But only of course if you are guided that way.

My love to you all,

Clare

And so, Clare kept helping with the work on the *Review*, reviewing books, contributing articles and replying to some difficult letters from readers. From her previous experience of editing *The Middle Way* and her own magazine she was well qualified in assisting Bert Hamblin in his task of running and maintaining the high standards of the *Review*. The benefit of her intuition and instinct with the affairs of the magazine was deeply appreciated.

In the spring of 1959 she left the cottage on the hill (Sophy her sister-in-law went her own way) and moved into a house with a landlady in Fairwarp. From here she continued to write profusely, visited friends and had guests to stay. Bert Hamblin was suffering from ill health and having hospital treatment for cancer. The responsibilities of his new position with the magazine were putting a strain on him and Clare's valuable input certainly relieved him of further anxiety. On 1 November 1959 Bert received from Clare:

Dear Bert,

Thank you for the most generous cheque this morning. It has been very strange — for a week or more I've been conscious of distress, though familiar when 'picking up' that of others, whether known to me or not. Quite a number of my friends have been afflicted one way or another — pushed downstairs, suddenly taken ill, and so on. Proper old battlefield!

Last night it seemed to reach some sort of crisis, as Love in me struggled to reach them all and really help. Suddenly I shot out of all the darkness, frustration, tension into — well, there are no words. I think it must have been you I was chiefly thinking of, and with blessed relief I knew Love was there.

The poem that followed doesn't convey the wonder of it, and only gives the merest hint, but may I share?

For some time I've guessed in a general way much of what you have been passing through, but these deep issues are sacred. We are on Holy ground. But the struggle *does* avail. Just as we know it is part of the preparation for the work ahead.

Forgive this, won't you? I feel so much happier to-day and feel you are, will be soon, more firmly on your feet in the deepest sense. The rest belongs to silence. No acknowledgment, please. May you feel that Love —

Sincerely, Clare

Love has taken all my songs
Consumed them in His fire.
The fragments scatter on the wind
That lifts the glowing pyre.

Love has taken all my songs
Bare now is the shrine
And broken all the idols that
I offered the Divine.

Love has taken all my songs,
But what are These, so bright,
In glory streaming overhead
With the speed of light?

Love has taken all my songs.
They know their bourne, not I.
Where sorrow's head is in her lap,
And tears fall silently.

Love has taken all my songs
And used them for His own,
And now on radiant wing they come
And go before His throne.

Love has taken all my songs
Bright powers to become
In His subtle alchemy
Now that I am dumb.

6

Deeper Communion and Greater Challenges

Though her physique was small, within Clare's body pulsated a driving energy which drove her on to accomplish greater goals. She always liked to be involved in many activities and meeting new people as well as fitting in daily, if she possibly could, vigorous walks over the nearby hills and valleys.

Walking in the beauty of the countryside had always helped her to attune to the natural rhythms of the universe and in nature she continued to find inspiration, refreshment and peace. She often spoke of being a gypsy at heart and loved to venture alone through the fields and woods, sometimes following the tracks which pilgrims had trod many years ago on their travels to cathedrals and holy places. She was much more content when lying down in a field, the grass for a bed underneath the canopy of the sky, than staying at home, restless and feeling confined. Out in nature at any season, her spirit felt at home, unconfined and deeply satisfied: "For we too are the stuff of leaves, and our blood the sap, and influences reach us from the furtherest stars as well as the more obvious sunshine."

She mixed with people from all walks of life — from lords and ladies to gypsies and men of the road; from painters, writers, poets, actors and musicians to innkeepers, game wardens, field workers, shop assistants and fishermen and many, many more. On a Saturday in Brighton in December 1959 she joined Mary Irene Curzon, daughter of Lord Curzon, Viceroy of India, and a life peeress in her own right (better known in those days as the Baroness Ravensdale) who was giving a talk on the relief of the world's refugees, a talk organized by the World Congress of Faiths, an inter-religious body which aimed to bring members of the various great religions of the world into greater fellowship. The next day she drank wine with a game warden whom she met in a country pub.

To Clare it was more important to go out first thing in the morning and walk over the dew on the grass than it was to open the morning letters. That beauty outdoors in the early hours gave her sustenance and inspiration to reply to her daily letters when reading them later. To stand and look up to the silver clouds rising into the upper domain of the sky filled her with a precious and magical beauty. Her heart was frequently quickened by some interior essence as she spent timeless hours in the company of the trees and flowers; that intangible essence which touches the soul from another dimension in which, when immersed, we stand in wonder and worship bereft of words. It was this larger vision of things, of which she was often conscious, that she held so close to her heart.

For Christmas 1959 she had a collection of her recent poems privately printed in a booklet; this she sent out as a gift to friends. She continued to repeat this gesture at Christmas for a number of years. Here is one such poem:

THE CHALLENGE

Above the hill crest of the snow
Where none but hardy reindeer go
I saw the ranks of verdant pine
Upon the early daybreak shine.

Taut as arrows, poised to spring
From the earth's green bow, and wing
Their promise whither? asked I then
Staring, from the world of men.

O dreams like spears, and powers divine!
Purified, and tempered fine
To pierce the skies, and bear the soul
Single, to the unknown goal.

O beautiful the flight the dares
Snap the silken nets, the snares
Beguiling in the flowery field,
The roof-tree warmth, the breast-plate shield.

Now, as a diver cleanly stands
With arms uplifted, clasped hands,
I go towards the verdant pine.
Its stance alert — it shall be mine.

And where the snow crest meets the sky

> Among the summon'd ranks will I
> Keep the vigil for that hour
> When breaks the Glory, and the Power.

In a letter to Bert Hamblin in January 1960 Clare wrote, after a snowfall the day before:

> We had about six inches of snow yesterday, now a slight thaw, but more in the sky. It quite intoxicated me, and I spent nearly all day out of doors in the sunshine and moonlight. The yellow flowers of the gorse shone like stars under their white burdens, and the moonlight was primrose over the snow in the early evening. Most beautiful ...

Her style and the coinage of her words in her poems, articles and letters was quite unique. Often her lines spoke of that eternal beauty which lies at the heart of all things. To the many readers who deeply appreciated her flow of words they seemed to be conceived in that sphere where angels and other sublime spirits live. They roused a great depth of feeling and yearning for truth and beauty in the awakened heart, echoes of a forgotten language known by the soul of man.

Clare believed that all work is prayer and that life became sacramental when we do everything for God. With such thoughts uppermost in her mind she lived, loved and worked.

With Clare's help, Bert Hamblin continued to edit the *Science of Thought Review* but his health was fading rapidly and the periods of radiation treatment which he was receiving became more frequent and necessitated longer stays in hospital. Through these difficult months Clare wrote many supporting and comforting letters to Bert to which he regularly replied with heartfelt appreciation.

On 24 September 1960, after prolonged periods of facing his illness calmly and fearlessly, Bert Hamblin died. He relinquished the editorship bestowed on him two years previously by his father, to Clare.

So, in November 1960, Clare Cameron became the new editor, a task for which she was well prepared. At the age of sixty-four, when most people retire from an active life, Clare entered a much fuller life, increased activities and a great responsibility which she faithfully carried for the next twenty-three years.

Eileen Carty, for many years the personal secretary of Henry Thomas Hamblin and business manager of the *Review* to this present day, remembers:

I worked with Clare as Editor until the time of her passing. Having worked with H. T. H. for a good many years I naturally wondered what it was going to be like working with Clare. I need not have had any apprehension. She was an ideal 'boss', always patient, kind and considerate and I can honestly say I greatly enjoyed working with her.

When I first met Clare at the funeral of H. T. H. I shall always remember how much I was impressed by the serenity that seemed to emanate from her though she admitted to me afterwards she did not always feel as serene as she outwardly appeared to be on such occasions. I found Clare to be a very tolerant person and never once did I hear her speak disparagingly of anyone. The office staff were very fond of her and would do anything for her. Her needs seemed to be very simple and one of the things she enjoyed immensely, as many of her friends knew, was to pack a small rucksack and set out for a marathon walk across her beloved Sussex Downs. On several occasions I would accompany her on these walks and though I was 25 years her junior and considered myself no mean walker she could easily outpace me! Then when we returned after these walks Clare would set about cooking an excellent meal. She was a very good cook and would often bring delicious home-baked cakes across to the office for the staff to enjoy. After our meal we would sit discussing the work of the magazine and topics in general. She could talk and advise on so many different subjects, simple and profound and was also a very good listener, unique in one who is often called upon to offer advice.

I, and the staff, will always be grateful for the years we were allowed to know and work with Clare.

The first article which flowed from Clare's pen in her new position as editor was this:

THE MIGHT OF GOD

Those who passed through the waters of sorrow and felt the support of the ocean of Divine Love which has cradled them, have felt this song of praise and joy welling up from within them as personal testimony. It is an inspiring, even awesome experience. They prove the power of the Holy Spirit to save, to take over the whole life in its infinite variety, its scope for pain and joy, its infinite potentialities towards goodness and happiness. Henceforth their refuge and their field of action are in God.

They give thanks then in the fullness of their hearts for the deep waters which not only supported in perfect safety but instructed them further in the Nature of God. Then indeed sorrow is turned into joy, for often, in the deepest sense, we find there cannot be the one without the other. Indeed, "He that is mighty hath done to us great things!" With infinite promise into all eternity.

But for this enrichment we find we have to learn of the sorrow in a rather special way, a spiritual way. Already we will have realised the folly of overmuch escape into distractions, which is the wordly way, sensible and helpful even as it is, up to a point. It is also true that time heals all things — up to a point. But we shall have missed a supreme opportunity for deeper understanding, for spiritual growth, for greater service to others, and hence remain the same persons as before, vulnerable to the next experiences of grief, anxiety, and so on.

There is no escape from suffering, for it is a fact of life. True, it does not *appear* to come the way of some, whom we may know only superficially, and who are blessed by health and wealth and all that the heart could desire. But often when you know your friends better you hear of 'skeletons in the cupboard', unknown behind the screen of those apparently easy lives. Often, quite suddenly, some calamity descends upon them and finds them quite unprepared, with no philosophy or faith with which to meet it. These are they who, bereft, reach out to their dear ones over the Border for assurance of survival, that they themselves here on earth may be comforted. This *can* be a subtle sort of selfishness. It were better, rather than seeking to drag them down, to try to live up to those they still love, that the Love of God may care for and teach them both, though one is still in time and the other beyond it. This brings an unbelievable measure of release from personal grief, into the joy of knowledge that all is a thousand times well with our dear ones, as it is with us also. We have entered into the realm of Divine Truth which is beyond our world, and which nevertheless shines at the heart of our world, and in the depths of our own hearts also. In that realm we are all the One Life which is eternal.

But it is not possible to have that experience of deep wonder, peace and bliss, until we can accept the possibility that at the heart of our sorrow *may* lie treasure, if only we can let ourselves be as helpless as a little child, and in faith that trusts where it cannot see, give over all to God in complete sincerity. We become emptied out, even as a jug is emptied of water; emptied of all self-will whatever its nature; submit to the cleansing, redemptive processes which surely take place and which we tend to misinterpret or misunderstand. For such is the make-up of the human mind, it tends to rationalise, to find a reason for everything which yet may be wide of the mark! So it is better not to question, yet to be very wide-eyed and attentive before God who is teaching, leading and working within us in His own secret and most beautiful manner. He is preparing us to be creative even as He is, to be a conscious expression of His Creation which is for ever taking place in the invisible.

Sooner or later, and that depends on our obedience and being prepared to go right through anything for God's sake, we feel that unmistakable quickening within, even as Mary when she sang her immortal psalm. And this is the awakening of our insight and joy. It is natural then to trust the ocean of Divine Love which bears us to unknown destinations. Having proved our own ignorance, we question no more, but wait in quietness always for the still small voice which is the echo of God's Voice within us. We need nothing more than that.

We will have shifted our centre of gravity then, understanding everything from a different viewpoint, and a much higher and wider one, too. Our lives revolve then about the new birth within us. It is our Light in all darkness, whose beams spread wide and far the more we live, move and have our being in that kindled radiance at the heart of our being. But we must tender and foster it also, naturally.

Not only in times of bereavement, but in sickness whether our own or of those we love, in all trials whatsoever, may we turn to this Treasure house whose capacity is able to meet all needs on all levels, spiritually and therefore most wisely and truly far beyond our power to imagine.

Here we come to other 'skeletons in the cupboard' that no one, no one at all, knows about, which we have kept hidden ever since 'it' happened, long ago. The betrayal and the hurt which never healed. Worse still, the betrayal of which *we* were guilty, and the remorse which has haunted us ever since, and the knife-thrust of guilt which never ceases to turn in the wound. In an old drama there was a famous line on which the curtain came down at the end of the act: "O God, turn back the clock and give me yesterday!" We echo that cry also.

We may not have even learned from our mistakes, but committed the same follies over and over again. "For the good that I would I do not; but the evil which I would not, that I do" (Rom. 7.19). It does not matter overmuch perhaps in the ordinary way, but when we have inflicted hurt ... the remorse never seems to heal.

We say we cannot forgive ourselves. No. Only God's forgiveness can do that, as only the Divine Physician can heal such a sickness which, if we are honest, is a form of self-centredness and a distortion of the truth. Could it be possible that we were the unwitting channel through which the friend received some necessary experience for *his* or *her* spiritual growth? Do we imagine that the appalling mistake goes on everywhere else except in our mind that refuses to let go of it, that refuses to move on? Have we so little faith in the power of the Divine Adjustment, that 'works in' *all* our mistakes as threads in the beauty of the Divine Pattern? And it is a Pattern which not only involves far more people than we realise, but is quite beyond our understanding. How dare we be so presumptuous as to assume that 'everything would have been beautiful if I (or so-and-so) had acted differently'? How do we know? Can we see farther than God Himself? We are as we are, in all the gradations of light and shade, in all the admixture of souls and personalities, and it is a step towards greater understanding and peace when

Two views of Bosham Harbour in the sixties

we learn to accept others just as they are, loving them just the same, *and* also ourselves.

While there is left one thing that troubles us, whether it can be great or small, or minute or major proportions, whether long-standing or recent, we have not given over everything to the Divine Physician, Teacher and Friend. True, it is not absolved or healed all at once, necessarily, though it can be, since the ways of God with us and within us are so subtle, so varied according to our capacity and need. I think perhaps it is so much easier to forgive others than ourselves. But if we are one in God, what is the difference?

He that is mighty can and does do in us 'great things', and there is no exception, except in our refusal to let go and know the blessed relief and release when we *know* that God really has taken over — everything. Such knots in the psyche, such deep hurts, may of course be in the unconscious and we may not even know from whence our unhappiness comes. But that does not matter, since we are known as we can never know ourselves, or others either.

It is enough to know that God whose kingdom is within us, forgives all things because when there is understanding, then lo, there is nothing to forgive. Therefore "the meditation of my heart shall be understanding" (Psalms 49.3). And help comes to us then, following our release from ourselves into the Greater Life, tangible and wonderful help from all directions. Wonderful because we know from *whence* it

comes, and we can sing with full hearts then not only the Magnificat, but "I know that my Redeemer liveth ..."

He lives in you, in me, for evermore, and Grace is abounding for evermore also, for those who seek the Lord in spirit and in truth.

Upon taking up her new responsibilities, Clare moved to a rented cottage on the shore in Old Bosham. Destiny had drawn her back to this special and picturesque part of west Sussex within view of the South Downs upon whose bridlepaths she loved to roam. Not long after her move she became quite ill with shingles and later on she often spoke about a rather alarming experience which she had at this time when, during the exceptionally high spring tides, the whole row of cottages where she was living was flooded.

With her enormous resilience she recovered from her bout of shingles, continuing to write and edit the *Review* in the midst of her weakness. After the death of Henry Thomas Hamblin, whom Clare often referred to as "an English saint in an ordinary serge suit", readers of the magazine fell away, feeling it would never be the same again. His son had, with Clare's help, struggled to keep the magazine alive but, hampered by his failing illness, it had been a great struggle. But with Clare's dedication, wisdom and writing gifts, readers gradually began to return. Daily she walked across the fields by the creek to the offices at Bosham House.

Her aims were to bring new blood and more personal articles into the *Review*. So the new phase began. The price of the magazine has never been raised over the years and it is supported to an extraordinary degree by donations. Innumerable and most touching letters began pouring in, welcoming her to the editorship. The hand of destiny had indeed now provided her with a special outlet for her innate creativity. Now she had the opportunity of touching nearly 7000 readers all over the world each month with her insight, understanding and the outpouring of her heart!

With many souls longing for a richer spiritual life, the purpose of Clare's life had, over the years, become more clear to her. Through her own orientation and experience she longed to reach such souls, to cheer and strengthen them, to help them to 'lay hold on eternal life'. With all her heart she sought to serve her fellow-man (to serve God), helping to awaken in them the nature of their true identity, their relationship with their indwelling divinity; the rediscovery of the interior life.

During the very cold winter of 1961 (Clare often indulged in reminiscences of this) the creek in Bosham became completely frozen over and looked like the North Pole. To save the life of many swans who have their habitat there, the local people broke holes in the ice for them and a nearby bakery provided bread. Through this act of kindness not a bird was lost.

After some time Clare moved to another residence in Stockbridge Road, in nearby Chichester, travelling to the *Review* offices each day.

Returning from a trip to Scotland soon after she wrote:

THE WHITE CALF

> Under the may-tree, freshly blooming,
> The little white calf with her legs tucked under
> Beside the track on the rocky hill-side
> Lies in the daisied grass
> And stares as I pass.
>
> This, and below, the clean white sheiling
> Down by the edge of the wide loch water,
> And every flower that receives her stumbling

Is all her world
As she lies there, curled.

All her world! The sandal of evening
Over the green of the mountain shoulder
Leaves a delicate footprint of silver
And points to the West
To the Isles of the Blest.

And for her music — O such sweet music
Of little waves lapping, the wind in the heather,
And over her head the sky-lark singing.
O man, attend her,
Sweet Christ, defend her.

Clare loved to travel and stay with friends; she accepted, whenever possible, any invitations to stay in different parts of the country or by the sea. Her visits to such places often gave birth to new lines of verse. She saw so much beauty, not only in nature but also in animals and birds and, of course, man. Through her poetry and writings she continued to awaken many others, increasing their sensitivity and perception to the beauty of life if we truly open our eyes and *see*.

Her favourite clothes were those of natural fibres; cotton, wool and sometimes silk, in rich colours of good quality, blending traditional styles with unusual ones from India, in particular. She was very much an individualist in her choice of apparel. Sometimes her pixie-like face peeped out from the folds of a voluminous cloak or she would stride across the Sussex Downs in cardigan and skirt or perhaps corduroy trousers, blouse and walking shoes. She also often wore classical clothes when attending special functions — well-cut suits or evening dress. When she walked into a room she was very much noticed, not only because of her appreciative taste in clothes but even more so because of her pleasant smile, sense of serenity and a special distant look in her eyes which spoke of another world far removed from the density of this material one.

Many years previously she had become a vegetarian. She wasn't primarily concerned with following a certain kind of diet as a means of knowing God, but she had come to this point through realizing that knowing God means knowing love and entering into the experience of a deep and abiding reverence for all life. Though she did keep basically to a vegetarian diet she wasn't at all rigid about

Bosham House, about 1965

doing so and accepted with gratitude what was offered when visiting friends. She believed it was more important to have a grateful heart for whatever was given (as all forms of life are from the same source), rather than draw more attention to herself by eating habits which were different from others. Above all, she often stressed that 'it was more important what came out of one's mouth than what went into it!'

She preferred natural, unadulterated wholefoods and loved to cook for others and bake cakes. She openly confessed to having a very sweet tooth!' She was also very liberally minded and liked to partake of dishes from different countries as well as more traditional fare. She was a lover of good wine, particularly home-made, and always maintained a philosophy of 'nothing in excess' which had been born out of her Buddhist leanings.

When Mrs Elizabeth Hamblin, widow of HTH, died in 1964 Clare moved to Bosham House where she lived for the rest of her life. Now that she was on the spot where all the activities of the magazine went on — the offices being situated a short walk across the lawn from the house, life was a little easier and she was able to receive the stream of readers who began to call. Friends visited, close ones stayed for invited periods and the foundations of this new phase in Clare's life were firmly laid.

Bosham House, situated in over four acres of grounds with views of the South Downs from the back of the house and a delightful view out over the waters of Bosham creek from the front, was ideally suited to Clare. She loved to spend time in the garden (partly cultivated and the remainder wild) amongst the many varieties of trees, shrubs and flowers, all planted by the Hamblins in earlier years. She shared picnics on the lawn and often slept in the summer-house under the moon and stars. The garden had a very special atmosphere which still remains to this day; this most likely came into being through the dedicated work which began here in the 1920s.

In September 1964, out of her heart poured:

SUN GOLD

The marigolds, rank upon rank, seem to embody, salute and radiate the glory of the sun like small reflecting mirrors. The tiger-lilies seem to proffer in their golden cups invisible wine. The yellow roses, golden at their centres, unfold like the very heart of love as we bend over them, offering the secrets of the Godhead, invoking the unfolding of the petals of our hearts. Here is communication, wherein the fragrance of the Divine may breathe forth from our own inmost centre, to help purify and heal the corruption in the world.

The air is fresh and diamond-bright in the garden in the early morning. Everything speaks to us. We recognise, worship and adore. Two of us sit there for a brief time, contemplating the Light, opening out to the Love, feeling the splendour and joy of the eternal that reaches to infinity everywhere, gradation upon gradation, arc upon arc, sphere upon sphere, and yet which is also contained in the marigold, the tiger-lily, the rose, in the sunlight and the very air, but locked up, alas, in the majority of living souls. Yet without knowing it, we are bathed in it, pervaded by it. . . . Rising from our chairs, we smile at one another in the communion of silent understanding. So are we charged with the very life of the Divine to take up again our daily affairs. How we long to communicate and share it, and pray that our hearts, mind and flesh may be obedient to its own sovereignty all day long, as channels for the flow of the Light and Love and the joy that is part of it. But all too soon the Sun-gold is dimmed and obscured, its all-pervading glory broken up into but tiny gleams as we make room for them in our consciousness. We thank God for the gleams, illumining from within the common-places of everyday as they can do.

In the evening, friends come. We talk of the purpose of art, which is to release the Divine through the brush, the pen, the sculptor's chisel, the bow of the violin or the keys of the piano, and the supple limbs of the dancer; all offered as channels to awaken a recognition and response in those who look, search, listen; making a way for the inspiration, delight and instruction from on high. We discuss the discipline involved, the training of hand and eye over long unrewarding years, the disappointments, the constant urge in the breast towards ever more true and pure expression that will not be denied. And this applies as much to a human life as the work of the artist. All work is, or should be, prayer.

One friend amongst us, confessing she knew nothing about art, said: 'I look at the way light falls upon the trees, or a landscape and am filled with longing. I want to be *one* with it all, to be identified with what I love so much. It nearly came through, once, seeing a sort of Biblical light over a flock of sheep in a field, so that I remembered Bach's lovely music to "Sheep shall safely graze"'. Another answered: 'That will come, and when you least expect it. We can but make a way for it to flow through.' Another added: 'We can be bridges, between the visible and the invisible. It's what happens in the apparently empty space between that is important, like the space in a room, or a door frame, or in the pause between sounds, or in the potent silences between friends. That is where the power is, as it is now.' And I thought: 'This is the inmost centre in us all, where the living, dynamic, creative truth abides in fullness.' For it takes place in *us*, and then the infinity of the within is seen in the without also, and lo, there is no difference. It is all One, where everything and everyone are most wonderfully and beautifully related, or would be known to be so, if we didn't spoil everything by our ignorance, analysis and interference.

Through our spontaneous conversation with one another, it seemed the very air tingled and shone with 'the bright shoots of everlastingness' of which John Donne wrote. It was like a net of Light in which we were all contained. We were 'all with one accord in one place', set free into the sparkle of the Light and Love. Here in a room at evening in the lamplight again was the Sun-Gold. Give thanks that it is everywhere! And can be released everywhere when we open to this Light and Love. For then it comes of itself.

The one who had first spoken, a very practical woman with little time for study or meditation, serving others all the time, said: 'Speaking of channels, I try to provide this in the street, in a bus or train — letting it flow into them, especially when a face looks strained, or sad. Sometimes a head will turn round and I have to stop.' She laughed. 'Rather embarrassing sometimes!' Yes, since the power can shake up and, for our good, disturb those discordant states of consciousness. Another then said: 'I suppose this is why so many people bring me their troubles.

...' and we discussed again the necessity for discipline, discrimination, balance in our service as well as in our everyday lives. Even channels have to be trained. How many aeons have gone to the making of the marigold, the tiger-lily, the rose, to all living things in the world about us? How many aeons to man himself, now crossing new frontiers of exploration in all directions, both within and without, and as it seems to some of us, in a rather lop-sided fashion in the materialistic, power driven (in many senses) age? We pray that the Holy Spirit within him may adjust, redeem, guide, even though it may have to be through tribulation if he will have it no other way. We pray that he may be lifted above the lure of earthly gold to the discovery of the Sun-gold which is within the Pearl of great price.

For surely this was implicit in alchemy, in the attempts to transform base metal into gold by the release of the Sun-gold (even as more evolved precious stones become transparent, which contains a profound lesson for us); in the search of the alchemists for the Elixir of Life; in the legends of the Grail; in the pilgrimages of all ages, as it is our own search still. Yet it is within us, and all about us, hidden and yet revealed to those who are prepared to earn their right to the keys of the Kingdom. *This* gold of joy does not fall into the laps of the unclean, the dishonest, the greedy, the slothful, the comfort-loving, the couldn't care less, and the majority unaware of their entanglement in the illusions of the world. It has to be earned, with infinite patience, humility and loving steadfastness, and in silence, and sometimes painfully. So our first steps are to learn, with the aid of the ever-present Grace of God, how we may be set free of such entanglements, and trained to be worthy channels.

For this our understanding has to be cleansed, and many cherished ideas which are our heritage from the past not only revised but some of them abandoned. They do but keep us down in the entanglements, and our vision remains partial and dim. We hear often in common parlance of 'the new look' applying to the outer form of things, in more colour in the home, new fashions in houses and gadgets, new approaches to the multiple social problems which whirl about us, and so on. Hence this is the appointed hour when the soul itself is called to 'a new look', reaching right through to the lower levels of ordinary living also, and it is only possible through a purified and more whole vision. It implies a *seeing* through the flux of phenomena and thereby helping to *bring* through the Sun-gold as it is in eternity obscured by the mists and motions of time.

Early man was a sun worshipper. Akhnaton (Amenhotep IV) of an early Egyptian dynasty about the same time as Moses, who believed in the one God and as a prophet of internationalism has been called by historians 'one of the most remarkable figures in the ancient world', in 1370 BC wrote a famous hymn to the Sun God which begins: 'Thy dawning is beautiful in the horizon of the sky, O living Aton, Beginning of life! So far back in time, yet wise and enlightened, he tried to interpret to his people and government the mystery, the potency and the spiritual implications of the Sun-gold. But the power of the priest-craft, the resistance of orthodoxy, were active even then, and he failed. So through the centuries the Great Divorce proceeded — between the flesh and the spirit, man on earth and God in the sky, so that only now is Christ's teaching of the integrating inner kingdom being recovered.

Yet man remains a sun-worshipper, and rightly so. Alas, that it is only his body on crowded beaches he offers to the sun, forgetting the ancient worship and wisdom ... seeing in the great luminary only something that is good for his health, fosters his crops, gives him light, warmth and material power. He has never been taught that our sun, one of countless numbers throughout the galaxies, is a mediating photo-sphere of yet another Sun behind it whose radiance would consume us if it were not screened by the wisdom of God. yet may it not be possible that what is behind and within the Sun, mystery upon mystery though it must necessarily be, has the power to illumine our minds, as reflecting mirrors, direct? We call it intuition, in-sight, in-spiration (for the rays of this inner Sun which derive from the greater open the petals of the heart so that it can perceive and draw upon heavenly air). Such in-sight, such in-spiration is more precious than any teaching from a book, unless the writer from a high and enlightened state of his own consciousness has that insight and inspiration. Then he can invoke our own, and help us towards the direct experience of it, the growth of it.

So it is not only our bodies that depend upon the Sun but our minds also, our minds freed of all doctrine and dogma, all conceptions, that they may receive this, this purified and *new* vision. Otherwise why did Christ tell us that the truth shall set us free; that He came to make all things new; and that He would send the Comforter to bring all things to our remembrance, i.e., the knowledge deep within our souls? But alas, for the distortion, the falsification of the ancient teaching through men, who harness still the Sun-gold for their own ends. ...

Atahualpa, sovereign Inca of Peru, was worshipped as a son of the Sun, and his kingdom was peaceful and beautiful. The conquistadors of Spain took the teaching of a militant Church to the pagans in the name of Love (today Communism calls it 'Liberation'). The sacred person of the king was killed, the Inca civilisation destroyed, the gold carried off and an unarmed populace enslaved. Nothing is now left after that shameful destruction in the early 16th century but ruins, and a mere remnant living in the high Andes in abject poverty and near extinction. You see, they were pagans. They refused to accept this travesty of Jesus Christ, lifted as a banner to cover the Spanish greed. They had to be subjugated, even as Galileo in his day who sought astronomical truth and nothing but the truth, even as the martyrs at the stake and the heretics in the Inquisition, even as until now murder on a vast scale was tolerated, if not wholly accepted, by the Church of our own day. Still we give lip service to the simple words, 'Love your neighbour as yourself,' but the practice of force remains. And we perpetuate it every time we seek to dominate, cheat or betray another, every time we cherish antagonism or intolerance, every time we are lacking in love.

Where O where is the Sun-gold that enlightens, heals and delivers, not necessarily from the evil of men, that has always been with us, but from the perpetuating of it? Right here, within us, streaming from its source in God, evident all about us every hour of our lives in the natural world, but unrecognised as it applies to us as channels.

A common cup or a crystal glass can still hold the same wine. A man is a man whether he wears a toga, a kimono, a skirt or feathers or a modern suit of clothes. Creeds differ, yet all teach Love and help us find Wisdom. Yet we have called all those who did not subscribe to orthodox Christianity heathens. We say they worship 'false gods', ignoring the fact that gods of our own day are acquisition of power, freedom to do as we like, lack of consideration for others, the grabbing of pseudo-gold in all its forms, to 'keep up with the Joneses!' and to 'be with it'. With what? Look about you and see the graven images on every hand, and then perhaps we can be a little more tolerant of those who worship the one true God under other names in the major religions of the world.

In fact, primitive tribes were more enlightened in some ways than we are, like the Hunzas of northern India, and as Laurens van der Post has found in his contacts with the very primitive little African bushman. For this shy little creature had more of the Sun-gold than we have. He had not experienced and suffered the Great Divorce, until he was hunted by modern man into extinction, leaving only his art upon the rock faces. Even very simple, almost illiterate folk radiate a happiness and contentment, an unquestioning faith that makes a channel for all who know them. Living on small means, they are essentially rich, for they live very near the Heart of God.

For we cannot command the Sun-gold as we can the earthly gold, since released within our imperfect vehicles and disintegrated psyches we should be consumed. Hence the neurosis and sometimes insanity that follows the pursuit of occult powers out of curiosity or for a new sensation, resulting in the inflation of the ego and unbalance. Then the Love of God is a consuming fire, purging away all that is not of Him before we may share, and pass on, His Wisdom and Joy. There is a very great deal in the world today that is not of Him, and much in us also, moral, virtuous and good-living folk though we may be. Hence we remain restless and, seen only from the outside, the Biblical texts that have served us well hitherto, now seem empty of meaning until we look deeper for the Sun-gold within them. It has always been there, all through the ages, from the beginningless Beginning, for it is the source of our immortality as our lives here and now. Even as the fragrance from the heart of the rose, the Grace of God emanates from the Sun-gold. When it opens up within us, we have the Elixir of Life of the alchemists, the wine of the Grail, the Living Water and the Bread of Life of Christian teaching, and under the direction of the Most High to Whom we are fully obedient, it pours through our humble, consecrated channels to meet all our needs, our own and others.'

There is much in music, poetry, art, the majesty of the mountains and the peace of green pastures, sun-rise and bird song, the mystery of birth and death and love that we do not understand. Yet all can, and do, give us a certain experience that is not quite of this world. Something reaches through and quickens us, and moves us deeply. It is as if a chink appears in time, letting through the Sun-gold, bringing us, however briefly, into living and thrilling communion with God's universe, nearer to God Himself as He is. It is as if we see everything as new, as for the first time, and it is new-minted gold. ... And underneath all the disturbing appearances it is coming into the world *now* with a powerful quickening. May we look for it, give it allegiance, and in whatever manner we are called to do so, work *with* it. For it brings a strange new joy.

Alec Barron, an astrologer, remembers well his contact with Clare over the years:

I first got to know Clare shortly after she became Editor of the *Review*. I never met Clare but once spoke to her on the telephone. She sent me her birth data just before she became editor, which conveyed much to me. On setting up her chart I realised she was a mystic and an inspired writer, as well as being practical at the same time, for she had the Sun and Venus in Taurus. She had the Gemini decanate of the 'New Age' sign Aquarius rising on her Ascendant, again emphasizing her writing ability. Her moon was rising in the second decanate of the pioneer sign Aries and no one could doubt Clare was a pioneer and a warrior in the Spiritual Realm. The second decanate of Aries is pictured in the sky by Eridanus — the 'River of Life' — flowing from the never-failing fountain of perpetual youth. Here we find Aries, ruler Mars is tempered by the magnanimity of the Sun, which has sub-rulership of this decanate. It is the Leo section of Aries and as Leo is the natural ruler of the 'house' of love so we know it bespeaks of the affectional influence *as well as* Spiritual Love. Only in the sacred precincts of Love does man quaff the elixir that imparts eternal life. So those born with this influence may seek this most hallowed source of power. The 'heart' is joined by 'head'. Clare's Sun was in the second decanate of Taurus so the fixity of purpose is given the analytical trend through the sub-influence of

Virgo. Therefore some condition in the environment is attacked, and made the centre upon which the physical *and* mental forces are focussed. In Clare's case she attained fame through literary production. The Leo decanate of Aries is pictured in the sky by Orion, the most successful of all hunters, who attacked and slew the mighty bull. The bull represents material pleasures and physical limitations, over which it is possible for those born under this decanate to rise supreme. They can mentally attack with a force as great as the huge club wielded by the mighty arm of Orion. They cause obstacles to crumble! The 2nd decanate of Aquarius which Clare has on her Ascendan.. was that of Pegasus: 'The Flying Horse', in other words the Gemini or Mercury decanate of Aquarius. The wings pictured in the symbol indicate the ability to leave the material body and travel in the super-physical realms either consciously or during sleep or both. Consequently she had unlimited resourcefulness in creative imagination and had the ability to convey her knowledge and ideas to others in the ideal way.

To Clare, astrology was a sacred science and she found the study of it helpful in understanding different personalities and aspects of the character, also the bringing to one's awareness inner potentialities, individual gifts and difficulties. One of her favourite books on this subject was *From Pioneer to Poet* by Isabelle M. Pagan, published by the Theosophical Publishing House, 68 Great Russell Street, London, from where she also obtained other works, particularly on reincarnation, karma and the evolution of Consciousness.

Other charts which Clare had done also confirmed the same aspects in her make-up. Ingrid Lind pointed out that part of her main work and task was to revive the consciousness of the far past and the truth such knowledge reveals; there was also much evidence in Clare's chart that spoke of her role as an 'awakener' or 'enlightener' which most certainly she was. Another astrologer indicated that she had the tendency to be too critical and too hard on herself and needed to relax, let go and love all of herself as much as she loved others. This was very true, as Clare had great difficulties in completely accepting and loving all the aspects of herself. Her Taurian will was very strong and sometimes got the better of her in areas of possessiveness and selfishness; this greatly upset her when she realized afterwards what she had been doing.

Mary Wonnacott retained some special recollections of her friendship with Clare.

It was in 1966 I found myself at Bosham House, working there on the staff and staying with our beloved Clare. I met Clare many years ago and was drawn immediately to her, experiencing oneness of the Spirit. I shall never forget this and the joy of being with her for 12 months was an experience which opened out my life in so many ways.

We were able to share so much of the spiritual and deeper things of life that meant so much and which helped me to develop a higher state of awareness of the Current that knows the Way. I was simple with my faith, and Jesus Christ was and still is very real to me today. Clare had her Buddhist Belief and this was so different to my approach and gave her more than I realised.

She was an artist and to watch her work was a joy. There were other occasions when we would go off for walks. I never knew what to expect when out with Clare. On one occasion it was a Saturday, a glorious day, lovely sunshine but I didn't realise that we would be walking quite a few miles in fact, it must have been 20 miles there and back! But this I do know, I was pretty depleted and exhausted for a couple of days or more after this hiking expedition. Clare thought nothing of it for this was her way of meditation and walking with God.

Walking across the Sussex Downs on this particular day was almost like summer, quite unexpected for the middle of February. The sun was warm and even the birds were singing. I well remember the wonders of Nature when we sat on the ground for a rest, looking around and viewing the landscape of Heavenly Beauty we both were aware of the Presence of God. So often this was my experience when in Clare's company. She was deep and words didn't matter, just to be in the Silence brought through so much of Divine Guidance, Wisdom and Joy.

There were other occasions when we would go off for long country walks. At one time I remember saying to Clare: 'I can't walk any more!' I don't know where we were but a gentleman was busy in his garden and Clare approached him asking if we could have a drink of water. And what a relief it was when the daughter very kindly made us tea. She thought nothing of climbing over hedges, going through farmyards for a short cut so as to get on the Downs. With Clare always something lovely happened — the beauty of Nature was greater, the sky became a softer blue whilst Mother earth a softer green. One learnt that something lived in every hue and that Christless eyes have never seen. And so I could go on like this.

To me, Clare was a great soul, she helped everyone that came to Bosham House and through this I've been one who was blessed the day she passed my way.

Another time whilst sharing an experience with Clare which I myself had had with her, she said: 'Mary, I want you to write an article for me on this!' I felt it was impossible to write on this matter but she insisted and pushed me into my bedroom to get on with it! Later that evening she came to see how I was coping but alas only to find what I had written was scrolled up and thrown in the waste-bin and I was feeling sorry for myself. She very quickly straightened out the papers and suddenly I saw tears streaming down her cheeks. She was so touched and delighted and said, 'This must go in the April [1966] issue of the magazine as an Easter message.' Through this I was able to write three more articles whilst staying with her.

Another friend to whom she was particularly close was Brian Gill. She felt strongly that they had known each other before in previous incarnations, such as mother and son in ancient Greece. He spoke of Clare in this way:

A very dear and close friend once spoke to me of the *Science of Thought Review*: this was about 1966 I suppose. She had just come across it and was finding it helpful in her daily life, particularly from the point of view of the book reviews which had opened up a whole world of contact for her but I could not allow myself to be impressed, having recently come through a protracted and bitter episode in relation to a spiritual teacher or 'Guru' during and after which I had felt quite devastated. It was with some determination that I resolved never again to rely upon or use as personal point of reference any source external to my own being. What could not be located within myself as a result of my inner journeyings and explorations I would from that point have to do without. A resolve that has held good through the years. And so I dismissed the *Review* and a little later was introduced to its editor immediately after a Buddhist Wesak Service in Brighton, I dismissed her too! I do not remember Clare's appearance on that occasion, a shadowy figure amongst shadows, it was clearly not our time to come together with recognition.

This was reserved for an event nearly a year later when I travelled to Chichester for a day gathering at which various people of weighty psycho/spiritual experience were addressing an audience of young people at a time in the '60s when there was a general awakening to the possibilities of higher levels of consciousness. Clare was not speaking on that occasion nor was she the chairperson, a role in which I was often to know her subsequently, but somehow, out of the crowd, we met. I suppose she was there representing the *Science of Thought Review*, there might even have been a stall of some sort nearby, I don't remember. What was clear was a sudden and real awakening to the presence of a very alive and vital person with whom I felt immediately in touch and at ease. It was as though we had always been old and trusted friends and that we were coming together after some long separation. Clare later confirmed that the feeling was mutual and we subsequently spoke of our coming together as a reunion. We chatted away and 'yes', of course I would come and see her soon at Bosham House and 'yes', of course she was right, I was indeed overshadowed by the spirit of Nijinsky. I had recently undergone a very powerful and unlooked-for psychic experience in relation to this great dancer and Clare, without any form of external knowing or reference, had picked this up. We parted sure that we would meet again. During our conversation, and in fact during the conference in general, communication was somewhat handicapped by the presence of pneumatic drills outside in the road. I remarked to Clare that they were in fact no worse than the constant noise of inner talking and emotional clamour that prevailed within the human psyche from day to day and which we accepted as norm. When the conference resumed Clare offered this contribution to those assembled and I was invited to stand up and develop the theme. I had in fact been speaking in public a little by this time but again Clare was intuitively sensing what was later to become my most important role and one of the more functional aspects of our future relationship.

She never lost an opportunity to promote my innate ability to put ideas into words and to communicate with groups of people and frequently she was at my side as chairperson whenever this was happening. Often we drove through the night together to some obscure hall or other, the meeting place of an earnest and sincere society of healers or seekers. She would sit patiently beside me whilst I did my best to create an island of contact and communication in a sea of empty chairs and bleak walls, badly lit by malfunctioning neon or naked light bulbs. But it was not so much our shared public life that I remember from our times together, for this was not the Clare that I came to know, to value and to love. Our relationship would flower into its own reality when the talks were over and on the return home we would stop the car at a roadside public house, where we would sit by a log fire and drink and chat about all those things that one reserves for close and intimate friends. On those occasions Clare would tell me aspects of her life I instinctively knew would never be for public sharing, revealing a personality and being quite different from that of the editor of a respected magazine.

Clare was never happier than when she was 'on the road'. Meeting people, often chatting to total strangers, making herself at home in surroundings totally unfamiliar and then moving on. She was ever open to the possibility of new contact and communications, to what she referred to as 'the gathering of souls' and since I am writing this account of Clare from the personal point of view I must confess that there were times when I felt our shared space and time together invaded and encroached upon. In those days I often had little energy when away from life's imperatives and necessities and would have been happy to stay longer with the glass of wine in a quiet corner closed in by our own private worlds of sharing, but Clare, slightly more than twice my age, would nod and smile in the direction of perfect strangers and soon they would be sharing with us the problems and difficulties of their lives. Then we would be up and off — to the Downs or the sea shore, 'Must have some fresh air!' Soon we would be battling against the inclement English weather in high places or close to the angry waves, buffeted by the winds and smarting with the cold rain that they invariably bore.

Of course we were undoubtedly out and about on more balmy occasions but these are not what come to mind in thinking of Clare. No, wild grey skies, sweeping landscapes, restless waves and the wheeling of flocks of birds in lonely places where the influence of man is less apparent are more truly the reflection of the Clare I knew. She was not a placid person, not a contemplative, indeed such a being could never have held together the vast network of connections that built up around her work for the *Review* and on her own personal account. She was used to authority and expressing herself through her contacts and influence. People like myself who dithered and tried to please were soon caught up in a mode of living that was innately Clare, a succession of short scenes enacted against a selection of backdrops into which could come all manner of persons from tramps and gypsies to the wealthy, influential and famous, to play a brief part and disappear, perhaps forever. The conference hall, the pub, the woods or open downs, the sea-shore, the meeting place of some group or society or the breakfast room of Bosham House, where Clare lived, were the locations against which I shared some of the sequences of her life. There may have been other settings but these are the ones I remember and of course the journeys by car in between. Clare always expected to have the car door held open for her and would not walk to a vehicle if there was any possibility of its being brought to the place she was about to leave, though once out in nature's open spaces distance was no object to her ever-eager feet.

She somehow managed to combine an innate propensity and command with a longing for simplicity and the shedding of responsibility, two aspects that caused her some degree of unrest and in the case of the former would, I suspect, prevent people from staying too close to her for fear of being inundated by her energetic and outgoing life. there were of course exceptions, people whose sense of identity was sufficiently secure to be able to meet Clare face to face as a personal friend and companion.

Perhaps Clare was the most generous of all the people I have ever met. She gave extravagantly and because of this always appeared to be immensely rich, though of course in material terms she had no personal wealth, not even the little 'nest-egg' that one would expect someone of her age and experience to have acquired. She did not seem concerned with personal financial security and appeared to have total confidence that, into the space created by anything that she gave, would flow even more, though I don't suppose she gave the matter any real thought.

For me personally her greatest generosity was in the sharing of the space in which she lived, together with her life itself. I always felt welcome there even when I arrived late at night and unannounced. And amongst the happiest memories of my life I count the times spent in the tiny living room at Bosham House, often with a tray of food balanced on my knee, with Clare and her companion Lorna for company. It was as though we met, 'came together', in one of the vestibules of eternity, but I never think of Bosham House as Clare's home. For me she was a person without a home. During the many years that I knew Clare the house remained the same — full of decrepit furniture inherited from the Hamblins and desperately in need of a domestic coat of paint. The plumbing was ancient and inconvenient and in winter the various stoves scattered around the house, in a vain attempt to hold back the icy blasts, needed constant attention for minimal results. I suppose Clare added to the clutter she had inherited in the house with a clutter of her own, paintings, drawings, stones from the beach, pieces of sculpture, china and so on not to mention a growing mountain of books, but she often expressed a deep-felt impatience with these acquisitions and with the demands both of the domestic routine and her typewriter.

She seemed to come truly into her own when the door of the house was closed behind her as we would set out on yet another excursion — an adventure of encounters in the world outside. Clare's nature, her essential beingness, was not easily contained. It neither looked for or needed a 'home' in the conventional sense of the word, though she was ever seeking those people and places with and in whom she could relax and relate with ease, though, as with so many of us, she recognised that in the deepest and most profound sense in the realms of time, space and substance there can be no home. Bosham House therefore was for me, and I think for Clare too, a station on the journey, a background against which we could meet and be together affording us a setting against which we could continue a dialogue immeasurably ancient, begun in other lives long, long ago for yes, to both Clare and myself, the existence of other lives that we personally had lived, in other bodies, was a fact beyond doubt or question. We saw our present lives and relationships against an immeasurably vast backcloth in time and space and in realms and dimensions beyond. It explained so much and particularly the recognition and ease with which certain things came together for us. It also brought pain when ancient, unresolved hurts came forward to be recognised and assimilated by a being overburdened by the sorrows that life in time, space and the material world can bring. I remember that the last time we were together we were watching the television. It was a film made in Russia and featured a difficult period of Russian history. We were both deeply moved and silently trying to contain our grief, each not wanting to impose it on the other but nevertheless aware of the profundity of the experience. At last we could contain it no longer and looked towards each other with tears streaming down our faces. With this openly acknowledged sign we came together to cry convulsively for a while and thus to release the pain. 'We were surely there,' said Clare, a fact which I had never for a moment doubted and which had recently been reinforced by my travels in that remarkable country.

We were both to some extent 'open' and 'psychic' and one never knew quite where or when this faculty would function, putting us in touch with accumulators of joy or sorrow in ancient buildings, streets, recurring events or tracts of open countryside. Of course our relationship was greatly extended and enriched by such encounters as it all made for a rich texture of sharing, especially as we would try at times to put some of the pieces together, to make a picture reaching far back into time. Much of our time together was shared with our dear and mutual friend Lorna who lived with Clare for many years. 'We were aristocrats in China together,' explained Clare when we first met, and who would have ever doubted it? When they were together one felt that gongs and bells, embroidered dragons, porcelain, jade and fine silk were never far away.

But more typically Clare, when left to her own devices was her gypsy self — a vagrant life that was never far away. She loved coaxing fires into life with twigs and bits of coal, an activity she could indulge fully in relating to the various primitive heating devices at Bosham House. She also considered a walk in the country incomplete if she did not bring something home with her. A bag of wild sea spinach for supper, a few sticks for the fire or an unusually shaped piece of flint; a propensity which has prepared me well for a subsequent friendship with an actual gypsy in Spain. How alike he and Clare are in so many ways; that same restless spirit contrasting strangely with profound insight and intuition born of a vision seen through eyes that focus beyond the horizon, whilst at the same time occupied with the essential trivia of mundane existence. How she would have loved the open and desolate landscape of my present mountain home in that country of sharp and powerful contrasts.

This is intended to be a personal view of Clare. Others will write of her tremendous sense of purpose and dedication, her service to humanity in the widest possible sense as well as through her work as the Editor of a magazine. I was always impressed by Clare's seemingly indefatigable energy and the ability to carry the considerable responsibility of her work at times when she felt wretchedly unwell and the way in which she would take herself to the typewriter, often late at night and with a house full of guests, in order to keep up with her considerable correspondence, giving comfort, reassurance and advice to the bereft, lonely and isolated when she was all of those things herself. Though there was a never-ending flow of visitors through Bosham House, Clare was always to some extent alone, separate, withdrawn, whilst at the same time manifesting openness and availability to a rare degree. For as with so many of those who travel the path of personal evolution and inner seeking, her life of personal relationships had seldom been easy and over the years it had brought her many losses. Yes, there were gains too but in the sense of deeply personal sharing of daily events and occurrences and the burdens of decision making. Clare had grown accustomed to being alone and had developed the courage and strength of will to cope with such a situation. Her soul companions, if she had any, were scattered far and wide and they met seldom or else, as one will see from her poetry, they were of the realms of nature or were to be found in worlds unmanifest where energy flows freely without the encumbrance of a physical body.

It was to such a world that Clare constantly aspired; her contacts with its heady heights made life at the mundane levels arduous for her. She felt an impatience that was never far below the surface though at the same time it did not manifest except where it would be understood and accepted by friends who were sympathetic.

Like Clare, I am a loner, though I have many good friends and even more acquaintances and have lived long enough to have lost many, one way or another. With a long grounding in esoteric knowledge and experience behind me it has, generally speaking, been possible to accept the passing of those with whom a close link has been established. Why then should Clare be the unique exception? Unfinished business perhaps? I don't know.

It is difficult to believe or accept that she is not there at Bosham House, thumping on her typewriter, opening tins of cat food, waiting at the front door in her red Tibetan-type hood and walking shoes for the car to be brought round, or poking at the redundant boiler fire. Though we talked long and often, there are still more things I want to share and a sense of a work unfinished, for we always felt there was more to do together even at our last meeting shortly before her death. Her passing from this world in no way diminishes this feeling. And so our dialogue continues, across the bridges and seeming barriers of time, of life and death and I have no reason to believe that it will ever be otherwise.

7

Out of the
Awakening Sixties

Enjoying the stubble. Late sixties

In the latter half of the 1960s a great surge of deeper exploration into 'man's search for meaning' and purpose of life took place particularly amongst the younger generation. This collective expansion of awareness and interest in the spiritual nature of life manifested itself in many of the young dropping out of the conditioned values of society in search of a better way of life in line with the teachings of Jesus Christ, Buddha and other great souls who have been given to us down through the ages. Gurus from the East and West appeared, attracting many thousands of followers to their teaching of that ageless wisdom; thousands of Americans burnt their call-up papers for the war in Vietnam in huge bonfires; flower-power was born — the way of peace and love; there was much global evidence of a great change.

127

Many in their quest for deeper meaning experimented with psychedelics such as LSD, mescaline, peyote, psylocybin, marijuana and hashish. Many of the young found these helpful in breaking out of the limited structures imposed by their own minds into more enlightened states of awareness. Of course they were also misused but to the sincere seeker in search of enlightenment they were instrumental in bringing many into a closer relationship with God and increasing their longing to spiritualize their daily lives.

With this awakening amongst the young, the pursuit and longing to know God more fully, Clare very much identified. Her own journey of awakening had been a different route but the goal was the same. She deeply understood the dissatisfaction and unrest amongst the young and the impetus which drove them in search of a more enlightened way of living. Recognizing this she opened her door and her heart to many of the younger generation who were passing through such a transition.

One such person to whom she felt akin was Muz Murray, as he describes:

By their very power of seeing deeply into the nature of existence, which brings them closer to the heart of life, mystics are often estranged from their fellow-men in the loneliness of their vision, uncomprehended by the majority of the world. Clare was no stranger to this problem. She once wrote to me: 'It may sound strange, but you know what I mean, considering the multitude of loving and grateful letters from readers every week, that for people like us it seems sometimes one is cut off and lonely, despite all one's various activities.'

I knew exactly what she meant. The deeper one goes, the fewer are those who can come with us. Thus it was that she and I became instant friends when we first met in 1969 despite the disparity in physical age and the fact that I was a long-haired bearded youth and a figurehead in the 'Flower-Power' movement of the time. But fellow-mystics recognise no cultural barriers or age limits. And there was something in our pre-Raphaelite-like mystical brotherhood which found an echo in the soul of Clare, which had been denied in her sterile Victorian upbringing.

In the rare instances when she was able to slip off from her duties to the 'dreaded desk' she would come to visit our community, Gandalf's Garden (a mystical centre in London) as gleeful as a truant nun, and revelling in the energy of the young around her, who were following a similar (if outlandish) path. Amid a congregation of 'hippies' and 'flower-people' she would say, with a naughty-girl gleam in her eye; If only the readers of the *Review* could see me now! Thus behind the scenes, she championed the work we were doing during the mystical renaissance of the world's youth.

Now and again, she would discreetly slip items from Gandalf's Garden magazine into the *Review*, as part of her many years of admirable effort to encourage a broader outlook among the many middle-aged and elderly patrons, without overstepping the bounds of possibility. But sometimes the limitations of those possibilities were a source of frustration to her creative and visionary spirit, which longed to reveal *everything* she knew as good and worthwhile. However, being in close intuitive rapport with the development of her readers, she knew just how far she was able to lead them.

She gave more of herself than many, but always felt inadequate in her giving, and had a tendency to self-deprecate her efforts. Sometimes the strain of her workload, the pain of her imagined inadequacy (a legacy from childhood) made her long for a retirement which was never to come. In such a mood she once wrote: 'O Muz, how I would welcome a complete change ... but I haven't a clue how, or when ... or why. I guess I still have a lot to learn about acceptance and non-attachment, since H.T.H. was right when he said we are always in the right place at the right time, though it doesn't always seem so to the rebellious heart that gets a bit frustrated at times.'

The 'rebellious heart' was never constrained for too long, and the Victorian repressed child which remained within her for life, was given its freedom now and again to do deeds of 'daring' it had never done before. I was amused once by her delighted 'revelation' that she and a couple of elderly friends had recently spent an afternoon smoking 'pot' (marijuana) in the garden and having a wonderful rapport with all of nature!

But the spectre of her dismally lonely childhood always haunted her in the background, creating an interior climate in which, try as she may, she was now and again visited by that dire affliction of spiritual aspirants ... the *Dark Night of the Soul*, in which everything one does apears to be utterly worthless. On one such occasion she asked me to write something on the subject for the *Review*, which I did. She responded by saying how helpful the article would be for many readers, 'just as it spoke to my condition, which is very trying at the present time. It feels like travail before rebirth into a new phase, and I can well understand why people who know no better commit suicide!'

It was such inner suffering and insight which made her able to help so many around her with great compassion. Whenever I went to stay with her, I found she was wasting away with giving, both in her writings and moving poetry as well as in her daily life, although she never felt it. Even passing tramps, to whom she endearingly referred as 'Gentlemen of the

Road' (and so they were) were housed and fed (by a time-honoured Bosham House tradition) for a few days' respite from the rigours of the road.

She would only infrequently allow herself the luxury of a few days off, and on some of those occasions she would do me the honour of selecting my company to 'recharge her batteries' as she said, by a mixture of metaphysical chinwagging, chanting and exchanging healing silence. Only a few of her friends knew of her interest in Hindu mantras (the repetition of Sanskrit syllables which have a healing effect) in which I played a part, as she requested my assistance for a personal mantra and the methods of chanting and breathing practice which we did together. Later she was able to find a yoga group near her home whose weekly chanting sessions she found 'very helpful, for it takes me back to a time before the origin of words'.

It was too many words which became a great burden for her in the last few years when it was evident that the 'dusk was gathering' around her life. Yet she struggled on, alternating between inspiration and exhaustion, sometimes succumbing to childlike fears of a future which never came, yet still inspiring others to the end.

In one of her last letters she wrote: 'I am intrigued by the title of the book you are writing, *The Dreamer Lost*, for that is what I feel myself sometimes, in the world as it is.' Although it was so, she knew the direction in which to go and her writings remain inspirational signposts along the way. I pray that my 'Dreamer' friend is no longer 'lost' but has now found the blissful rest she so surely deserves.

Clare had a special ability which enabled her to communicate with those many years younger than herself; in fact she found communication easy with people of any age. She was very open-minded and young at heart and felt just as much at home sitting sharing experiences on a cushion on the floor with young long-haired men and women as she did at a polished oak table, sipping tea from fine bone china with titled friends. She tried marijuana to experience the effect it had on one; attended concerts by musicians such as the Incredible String Band; joined in peace gatherings and full-moon meditations held by different groups and played with children. She was very aware of the expansion of consciousness that was unfolding in the younger generation at this time.

She loved music and amongst her record selection were albums from such renowned composers as Mendelssohn, Beethoven, Vaughan Williams and also India-influenced musicians such as Quintessence and the Incredible String Band. She was very fond of the songs and music from the hippie musicals *Hair* and *Godspell*. She liked Chinese classical music and records of British birdsong. Her taste in music covered a wide field from the classics to the very modern and unusual but always she looked for the inspiration and beauty that each expressed in their own way. She was always open to new and alternative forms of creative expression as well as older ones and was very much a bridge-builder between the old and the new.

In her editor's notes in the November 1969 issue of the *Review* she shared:

MOTHS TO THE FLAME

In these Notes we are going to ask one another how we are meeting the uprising of youth in our time and whether our attitude is one of sympathy, condemnation or just uncertainty and bewilderment.

It has been said there is nothing new in it, since in all periods youth has sought to be 'different', aggressive as it has fought to have its opinions listened to, and as a compensation for its immaturity; rebellious towards adult authority; a little flamboyant deriving from instincts to attract the opposite sex; ambitious or idealistic to the age of the soul in those young personalities; and so on. But we venture to suggest that this uprising going on all about us, is different, and far-reaching in its implications and possibilities, both good and not so good.

Looked at in one way, it is the pendulum swing from what we, the older generation, have taken for granted for far too long in our apparently helpless acceptance of violence, competition, humbug and hypocrisy. The young are breaking all that appertains to the old order in their ignorant and often unwise attempts to release the new. There are criminals, thugs, lazybones evading responsibility amongst them, but there may be pioneers, teachers, and even saviours. They will not accept something as valid and workable because authority says so; they have to find out for themselves, and they are doing it somewhat wildly, but fearlessly, and their numbers are growing. This is an incoming tide that cannot be stemmed. Are we going to try to understand them, and from that to give some sympathy, or to condemn as many are already doing?

Set in our ways, supported by traditional standards, fearful for these young feet exploring dangerous ground (especially those who are parents), we would bring them back to what we consider normal, incredible to our forefathers, such as the aeroplane, television, computers and all the technological devices and discoveries of our age with their application towards 'progress', we now take for granted. The foundations of yesterday are the jumping-off grounds of today. So it will always be.

So naturally the young will not be brought back into the old tracks. When we were their age, we dared not question much that was vaguely felt to be wrong, untrue, and sometimes shameful, but unless we were revolutionaries or anarchists, quickly we became conditioned, our fresh vision blurred, the heart's glow fading as the years passed. How else could it be, when adults were supposed to be wiser, more experienced than we were, when there was a career to be won, a family to be maintained, security to be kept at all costs? Here and there amongst us, the visionary may have asked if the sacrifice was worth it, for we too sometimes found stones instead of bread. And do you remember the teaching about hell-fire that was held before us when we failed to accept and obey parental authority? The founder of this magazine, our beloved Henry Thomas Hamblin, suffered from it for years, as he tells us in his *Story of My Life** and his articles, until *he* had the courage to *think* everything out for himself and break away from such pernicious doctrine. He was a pioneer fifty years ago, and helped to an immeasurable degree to release us. You will remember other examples, and in this sense the youth of today compare favourably with those of even thirty years ago, despite appearances to the contrary.

Then think of all that is being done by the younger people in increasing numbers, schoolchildren amongst them, for the aged, the helpless and the homeless, the down-and-outs, the rejects of society, the drug addicts, hastening *in most human ways* the urgent reforms where Governments lag behind, such as Shelter, the Simon Community, Task Force, St. Mungo Community (Soup Run), Christian Youth International (new generation movement, known in Europe and Asia as Gen, which has already quickened the imagination of 80,000 youngsters), apart from the bigger bodies such as Christian Aid and others, and solitary individuals like Sally Trench. Their numbers grow, thank God.

But what of the others, the hippies, the beatniks, the flower children, the young squatters, who are also breaking free? Some of us are appalled, because their kind of freedom seems not liberation but licence, and a frightening licence at that.

Here too let us take a look at the old tracks, still well-trodden by the majority, of evasion of the major issues of our time, selfishness, greed in however small a degree, cruel competition that is partly responsible for the mounting suicide rate; sporadic wars over the face of the earth any one of which, any day, may burst into a flame it will not be easy to quench; slavish adherence to convention, both sacred and secular; the gross inequalities that provoke economic upheavals in all aspects of

*Published by the Science of Thought Press Ltd, Bosham House, Bosham, Chichester, W. Sussex PO18 8PJ.

national life; the emphasis on 'rights' instead of responsibilities; the rampant materialism which is at the root of much evil and to which even the most intelligent succumb to some extent, the decline of religiosity that has not yet broken down sufficiently to reveal not only its weakness and falsity, but the inspiring vision of religion which will no longer be merely a creed, but *a way of life*.

Now let us consider the new tracks already appearing in our midst being made *for* us, faint and twisting and appearing to go in wrong directions as they often do. Along them we meet a fearless enquiry, the courage of new outlooks, new attitudes to all that passes for 'life' but all too often is mere existence. We meet harmlessness instead of violence, love instead of hate, lack of possessions instead of too many that engulf the spirit, a refusal to become involved in 'the rat race' since its prizes turn to ashes eventually; an idleness that appears to avoid responsibilities but which does allow time 'to be'; gentleness instead of aggression, innocence that has not yet been corrupted.

What; not corrupted? Look at the mounting tide of promiscuity and drug-addiction in our permissive society. You may retort that if that is not corruption I'd like to know what is! But what of the mounting tide among adults of sleeping pills, tranquilisers, palliatives, pep pills and so on, the drugs of mechanised entertainment, of the Press, sensation seeking of all kinds, and much else that inhibits straightforward, honest thought and avoids direct experience? And is promiscuity only practised by the young? Could it be that we are just as trapped in the jungle as this strange new race of modern youth?

We know that large numbers of them are attempting short cuts to religious experience (youth is always in such a hurry anyway) and alas that the commercial market and political groups exploit what is fundamentally a search for Light. And so feeble on the whole is the Church to understand and help them (set in its ways) that we can hardly blame them for the short cuts through drugs. They have nevertheless genuine meditation groups, following the influence of the Maharishi, even though some do not know what they are meditating about, and we are aware of the dangers here. Their pop songs, despite the raucous impact on unaccustomed ears, when we give them unprejudiced attention are sometimes evocative of the visionary gleams we once had and, dare we say it, sometimes nearer to the simple teaching of Jesus than some of the old doctrinal hymns. They have their own magazines which are so alive that they remind us of new shoots putting forth from the dead wood which a few of us, in the older generation, have found unsatisfying for some time. There seems so little in that dead wood to quicken the spirit. In these magazines you find announcements of reputable groups and societies, Buddhist, Theosophical, Vedantic, Yoga and others eager to welcome these young people, including the Quakers who give them a warm welcome in their Meeting Houses. If you give them a lift on the highway, sometimes you meet beneath the odd make-up an unexpected charm and culture that is refreshing and heart-warming. One of our occasional contributors recently speaking at a serious Summer School in Paris was moved by their spontaneous affection on her departure. She, and others among our readers, welcome them into their homes. And how grateful we are for this welcome, these attempts to understand and help and guide ... for how needed this is.

As I write, on a warm night in late September, a little silvery moth flutters in from the dark to the lamp, and I am reminded of these boys and girls who, seeking illumination (many are, you know, despite the others) about the truth of things and the purpose of life, are in danger of searing tender fragile wings. Like the moths to the flame, they do not know where they are going, only that instinctively they seek Light. Perhaps it is better that they do not know, yet.

The instinctive in the unconscious, even the superconscious, when free to act, has its own wisdom. These young creators of the future are not yet in-formed. How could they be, in such a time of transition, moving across quicksands of uncertainty and experiment, through deserts where too often they are offered stones for bread? Are they acting as buffers between the old order that is passing and the new not yet come, steadied by the relatively more normal young people referred to earlier on in these Notes?

What is going to happen to them? We do not know; we remember all that has happened so swiftly in recent years, needing fresh questioning. and so if we do not know — and who does? — let us at least be willing not to condemn out of hand, out of ignorance, because we are set in our ways and reluctant to forsake such attitudes for the uncertainty of the unknown. We can send even the most scruffy, lazy, violent, irresponsible drug-addicted amongst them our love, our prayerful protection: are they our enemies, threatening decent standards, all that we hold of 'good report', as we continue fearful not only for their own salvation, but our rocking world? Is it faintly possible that, immature and groping as the young are today, they may be helping to create a new morality that is nearer the teaching of Jesus than ours, a new religion of experience, not theory? This may of course sound fantastic, now.

We pray that new leaders and teachers may arise, who already may be amongst us, able to interpret the teachings of the great religions in ways they can accept and follow, since many of the well-worn disciplines are distasteful to them, and for good reasons. We have to meet this new fourth-dimensional seeking, for that is what we believe it to be, that leads to the More Abundant Life, the Life of Grace which some of us have already so joyfully discovered. We cannot meet such seeking with the old three-dimensional consciousness and methods, of man-made laws, man-made morality, where the tracks have become overgrown through the centuries. Perhaps, in a sense, we can travel with them, and that will help them and mankind most. Meanwhile, let us pause and examine our hearts. Let us judge not, lest we be judged.

As we go to press, we may have been disturbed by the recent outbreaks of violence which got completely out of hand, and which damage the reforms originally envisaged and planned. Mass hysteria begins with a minority, and then drastic methods of control are the immediate, if not the ultimate answer. Not once but several times in these pages we have suggested that under the present spiritual out-pouring the tare and the wheat are growing up together, that the 'bad' is being thrown to the surface for a major cleansing even as in a patient with fever-releasing toxins. There has always been violence in human nature, but only now are we made more aware of it through a sensa-tional Press and its encouragement on our television screens. As yet, all that is happening to bring the Kingdom of God more evident on earth does not 'make a story'. Where possible, let us seek to cultivate a better sense of values and recognise the power of thought to enlighten the distressing ignorance of the majority.

Let us seek to foster the young shoots struggling to find their way among the tares of this emerging young generation, despite those who, in their own ranks, betray them.

I first came into contact with Clare in 1969. Earlier that year, whilst going through a transitional period in my life, a friend gave me a pile of *Science of Thought Review* to read. I was twenty years old and living with Fif, my wife to be, in a rented flat in the seaside town of Folkestone in Kent. Since I was fourteen I had been searching for a deeper meaning to life. I left my home in Ireland at seventeen in search of something more! During my search for that 'something more' I had experimented with psychedelics which served to deepen my awareness and sense of purpose; undergone a series of mystical experiences and expansion of consciousness which had begun to change the direction of my life. I had been living a hippie lifestyle and was beginning to realise the futility and danger of using psychedelics to enable me to remain in a heightened state of con-sciousness; giving them up I had begun to explore and practise different forms of meditation and self-inquiry.

I was in a very over-sensitive and vulnerable state when I first came across the *Review* and, on reading the articles by Clare and Henry Thomas Hamblin, I was filled with excitement and a great relief — here were two enlightened souls who clearly spoke of the awakening in consciousness which I was going through, in ways which I truly understood. Being a lover of verse, I was particularly touched by the very vivid and poetic way in which Clare expressed herself in her poems and articles whose content confirmed the yearnings and questions of my deepest aspirations. In Clare I immediately felt I had found a wise elder member of my tribe and felt very close, as if I had always known her. The contents of the *Review* seemed to meet a deep need within me and I sent a subscription to receive regular copies. I felt as if I had found a lost link on my journey back to God.

Each subsequent copy of the *Review* provided much nourishment for the hunger of my soul. Some months passed, Fif and I were married and, at the end of 1969, our son, Kaladin, was born.

In 1970 I wrote to Clare (omitting my address — I was then living in London) expressing my gratitude and appreciation of the *Review*. In the October 1970 issue of the magazine, she replied within its pages:

> Dear Brian, Fif and Kaladin,
>   Thank you for introducing yourself and your wife and little son, and for your appreciation of our *Review*. Not only you, but many readers, often feel "like a candle flame almost extinguished in these days of storm"; but I am glad you also feel "the breath of the Creator of All spreading out from within and filling the hearts of all with love. For Love is the essence of us all" and how right you are. Also I appreciate your saying "for in being ourselves, and in learning the lessons we have returned to earth to learn, it matters not what your appearance is" (such as your long hair and sandals). "It is what is in your heart that counts, and the practice of the laws of The Creator of All Things in our daily lives." You have a poetic touch when you suggest "we are tiny twinkling jewels, stitched together with the same thread in the Cosmic Pattern of the Infinite Being's Gown". Your closing prayer is: "May the love that has given life to us all, awaken us, and clear away the cobwebs from our dusty eyes!"
>   There are a few whose eyes are not all that dusty, dear Brian, Fif and Kaladin, and into that happy company we bring you, and as you render to others the small services you have mentioned, we wish you all blessing, and all manner of Good.

And so the foundations of a very close and special friendship between Clare and myself were laid, a friendship that had its beginnings before our present lives and the roles we played. It was a

coming together of two seemingly separate units whose individual
destiny was to be closely interlocked and woven in the tapestry of
time in the years to come.

Neither of us realized then, the periods of change and transition
which lay ahead; the results of these were to foster and deepen our
relationship, bringing us ever closer together not only in the
hallowed haunts of sharing which are experienced in such a friendship but also in a joint working relationship providing us both with
further opportunities to serve our fellow-man.

From the very first contact, I felt intuitively that I had found a
long-lost friend. I shall never forget the heartfelt feeling of gratitude that welled up on numerous occasions in the years since that
first contact and will forever keep on doing so.

We continued to write regularly to each other, sharing our
deepest feelings and what we were going through but it wasn't until
the summer of 1971 that we first met.

My wife, Edith my sister and I had opened our own business
(Deva Wholefoods and New Age Books) earlier in the same year
when we had returned to Folkestone to live. We discovered that one
of our customers was an old friend of Clare's. This gentle lady
offered to pay for a hired car with driver to take us all to Bosham
House to spend the afternoon with Clare; we very gratefully
accepted having no transport of our own at the time.

I remember walking across the lawn on that hot summer's day
and there before us was a small, slight lady with Tibetan features,
grey hair cut in pageboy style with arms wide open in welcome.
We embraced and, looking into Clare's eyes, I saw a special light
and wisdom there and my heart was filled with a 'coming home'
feeling.

Clare's companion, Lorna Clayton, was also there. I particularly
noticed the bright sparkle and joy that emanated from Lorna's eyes.
She was dressed all in yellow with a straw hat and, like Clare, there
was a special feeling of warmth and understanding that poured
unrestricted from the depths of her soul.

Lorna had been living with Clare from 1970 and one could
immediately detect that they shared a close and precious friendship.
Both of them seemed like two wise old souls (not in a physical
sense) who possessed a hidden knowledge not known to the
majority of men. They made us very welcome and delighted in

Kaladin's spontaneous communication and toddling exploration of the house and garden.

We all shared a lot that afternoon in our conversation and in silent pauses and when it was time to go we bowed to each other acknowledging the divinity in each other's heart. I departed, filled with a much greater sense of direction, God's love and clarity of purpose.

From that very first meeting I was acutely aware of the rarity and depth of communication that flowed so easily between Clare and myself, not only when we were engaged in verbal communication but especially when we sat in silence in which the communication between us continued to flow. In Clare I had found a very special and unique friend; one who understood my deepest yearnings and with whom I could reveal *all* of myself. I felt so uplifted and deeply grateful to the ways of God who I felt had brought us together. On the journey home my heart sang a song of gladness and upsurging joy.

I was deeply touched on reading in the September issue of the *Review*, Clare's own impression of our meeting:

> We had corresponded but never met, until the hot summer afternoon. An elderly elegant lady had paid for the hired car that brought them many miles across the country. As they walked across the grass — three beautiful young people, a little boy and the lady, they brought an atmosphere with them that was most noticeable. How to define something so intangible, that seemed to make all that engages the attention and the time of the average person so trivial, almost vulgar? Yet it was only that they brought a quietness, a simplicity, a dignity that was like a fragrance from another world.
>
> They are not remote from it, for they earn their living, and therefore Sunday was the only day possible for them. As we talked over the teacups, sharing experience, one realised how vulnerable and sensitive they were, like so many young people, feeling their way through the mazes and impacts of our time with only their spiritual instincts to guide them. This was a relief, for the consciousness in which they seemed to move, apart from what was said, would take care of them, apart from their simple, gentle, unstressed dedication which was obvious. They talked sense, but it was spiritual sense. Yet more than their words, it was this *consciousness* pervading them from which I was learning, in which I was partaking. How they will smile when they read this! Yet it was so. They were only able to stay two hours, but how much was conveyed in that brief time ...

Afterwards I began to wonder what it was they had that we have lost, looking for it in our books and studies, in our spiritual techniques and disciplines, what it was that they seemed to have *naturally*, like certain other young people today moving amongst us. I wondered how *we* might recover our quietness, our simplicity, our dignity in a noisy, chattering, frenetic world.

And I thought of the Noble Eightfold Path of the Buddha, the middle way between extremes, the steps of which include Right Attitude, Right Conduct, Right Speech, Right Livelihood, Right Meditation and so on, all being branches of what we might call the Tree of Original Virtue, or in Christian terminology, the True Vine in which we are rooted and from which we break away at our peril. It is also the Tree of Life which nourishes, tempers and balances every thought, desire and deed, and once it germinates and begins to grow within us, it becomes embodied also in our physical vehicles, with restored health of body, mind and soul. Though its crest is the Light, its roots draw strength from primal energy, which depth psychology teaches.

However, this is not the theme of these Notes but rather to draw attention to but one aspect of the Noble Eightfold Path, of Right Speech, beginning with a greater awareness of our chatter, most of which is not only unnecessary but dissipates energy, as well as adding to the clutter and noise all about us. It is hardly intelligent to complain about the jets overhead, the neighbours next door, the traffic on the roads, and all the other noises which so far the Noise Abatement Society seems unable to lessen, while we are adding to it however slight a degree, Listening to the quiet voices of the young people that Sunday afternoon, and aware of the *quality* of the conversation, it seemed we all have something to learn about Right Speech . . .

In Clare and Lorna, we too had found a special quietness, a simplicity and beauty that spoke from behind words. I was also conscious of a very healing and peaceful presence which seemed to pervade the very air around them; of the love that made us feel at home and of the beauty and sensitivity that was expressed in many little caring ways.

The door of Bosham House was ever open for the constant visitors and, no matter who they were, be they writers, poets, healers, spiritual leaders, readers of the magazine or whoever, Clare always gave everyone a very warm welcome and practically every visitor left with something she gave them. These were not only gifts of her understanding but other gifts such as a book, some inspired and helpful piece of writing, some fresh-cut flowers or vegetables from the garden or perhaps a household item of which they were in need.

Ian Dickie, a Canadian reader of the *Review* who visited, remembers:

> I have quite a pleasant memory of Clare Cameron. I drove diagonally across Sussex from the extreme north-east corner around East Grinstead or Fellbridge to find Bosham House. Got lost around Bosham harbour and the tide came in covering the road.
>
> Finally I located the house behind the then new road. Well, Clare came over in her carpet slippers and I ended up leaving with a tremendous bunch of sweet peas and a huge bag of beets straight out of the garden. So you see Clare had more than words and paper to give. I always appreciated that little visit ...

As well as being a supportive companion to Clare, Lorna also drove Clare to many outings. They both loved to go on jaunts together into the countryside with a picnic or journey to an out-of-the-way country pub for a ploughman's lunch or to some other meeting, a play, musical concert or to visit friends.

On making visitors feel welcome in her home, Clare wrote:

IF YOU COME ...

If you come into my house
You come into my heart
Where all is not as it might be
Even though beauty is here
And an aroma of peace perhaps
For all who understand.

A home takes on the qualities
The subtleties of atmosphere
If you disregard the shabbiness
Where all is not as it might be,
You may feel it, and disregard
The rest, and I thank you.

If you come into my house
You come into my heart
The door is open for you
And you are always welcome,
If you will take it
Sympathetically, simply, as it is.

She loved having guests, baking sponges or flapjacks for them and serving tea and always having time to listen to another's problems, giving support and understanding and sharing her own. She was a special and trusted friend to many.

One of the most beautiful poems she wrote on friendship was:

FRIENDSHIP

Whether we meet alone or in company,
Engaged in the trivia of conversation
To tinkle of teacups and laughter,
Meeting the needs of the moment as birds on the wing,
It makes no difference.

Whether I catch your eye as we walk in the woods
That sees what I see of beauty, revelation,
Or you take the hand of my friend in the drawing-room,
And years may pass before I see you again,
It makes no difference.

In Spring the leaves dance on the bough,
In Summer the tree gathers her skirts about her.
In Winter the white hands of the snow
Suspend, forbid, and lock her in silent embrace.

The gifts of love as the gifts of life
Cannot be grasped and yet they cannot be lost.
Hearts may break and hope splinter to fragments,
To what is between thee and me eternally,
It makes no difference.

Her days continued to be very full with the responsibilities of the magazine, her writings and receiving visitors. Whenever she could she would be off to a conference, lecture or pilgrimage such as the ones arranged by the Wrekin Trust (a charitable foundation founded in 1971 by Sir George Trevelyan and concerned with the adult education of the spirit). Clare particularly liked to attend these conferences because of the opportunity such gatherings offered for different people with similar interests to meet and share. It was at such activities that more friendships were cemented.

Eileen Churchill recollects:

Clare first came into my life when she attended the first Summer School arranged by the Wrekin Trust in the North of England. It was an event arranged by me at the Northumberland College of Education of which I was Principal, during the summer vacation. I was thrilled by the response from all over the country which included people like Winifred Rushforth, Mary Swainson, Patrick Blakiston and Theo Gimbel. Among them was a small, self-effacing lady of whom I had been in awe throughout the Summer School and particularly in appreciation of the zest with which she partook of the drama session. We were studying the spiritual journey of Odysseus.

Towards the end of the Summer School Clare told me about the *Review* and asked if I'd like copies for myself and the college. I said "yes please" and from then on received three copies. One went into the Quiet Room at the college, one was handed on to a member of the Meditation and Healing Group which was started shortly afterwards and now meets in Newcastle since I retired. The third I've handed on to people who I thought would appreciate it.

After that first meeting I met Clare often at Wrekin Trust events and we always found time to be together. I felt immensely privileged when she wanted to share with me many of her personal sufferings and glad that she felt consoled by the sharing ...

Dear Clare, we loved one another and I learned so much from you. We learned to listen to each other, to share our deepest concerns about the world, the Universe and the Cosmos in which we live and move and have our being, and which we are called to serve.

I found you a shining example of devotion, integrity with a single-minded love of Truth, goodness and beauty, which I can only hope to emulate if I am fired by the same zeal.

> Your shining star in a grey world
> Gives us courage to hope and to serve.
> Your twinkling star in a disordered world
> Gives us faith to endure and to serve.
>
> Your brilliant star shows us the way
> And continues to inspire us.

Clare also went through disturbing times of inner turmoil as do many who aspire to greater heights of understanding. In a letter in January 1975 she expressed some of the difficulties she was experiencing:

Dear Brian,
   I meant to thank you for your last letter long before this, and to say that indeed I think some of us *are* being tested to the utmost, everyone differently according to where we are most vulnerable. I get terribly irritable and 'on edge' with bouts of black depression which apparently others have, and as if one is still waiting for something. Often it feels as if one is in labour and if it's a rebirth then it is long overdue! Outwardly

there may be no reasons for it since "all is taken care of" most marvellously. But perhaps we are sharing in the travail of the planet. One can only trust the higher consciousness which sees the way and is always serene in that knowledge.

Many more new friends are being drawn to Bosham House, as if we are being gathered together in this time of urgency.

I never realised how much self-will there still is in me, and how much egotism calling for utter submission to God and utter trust. So glibly one can write of surrender while only knowing it mentally. One has to accept all one is and release it . . . easier said than done in tough characters like me!

How I sympathise with you in the restlessness, for I swing constantly from nervous tension to fatigue, and scarcely know myself these days, but it is happening to many souls, and we are carried through.

It also seems a time of waiting, but I feel we are being prepared inwardly, though I do not find it easy to co-operate. One goes on feeling so frustrated, so it is still a time of testing but we are safely led along the knife-edge.

> Always love to you,
> Clare

In another letter she said:

Dear Brian,

O how I echo your words that "the more peace I want for myself, the more people and activity come along!" It seems some of us are called to sacrifice much (opportunity to serve) that others find necessary. Like me, I expect you'd love a holiday and a break from the routine, but in these urgent days perhaps the harvest is great and the labourers are still few.

Bosham House seems to become more and more magnetic — friends here every day this week, so the 'gathering of souls' proceeds swiftly. Life becomes more and more of an adventure but rather exhausting!

I do find it difficult to relax under the impact of these new spiritual energies, swinging from acute tension to exhaustion. Others don't seem to be nearly so affected! And yes indeed, though I have no children, it must be similar to the pains of labour, for at times one feels the quickening of a new birth within, and increasing sensitivity to the power of the Spirit. But at times it's almost too much, especially upon all in oneself that is so unregenerate. So I suppose it is the fire of purification that we are also passing through — perhaps this is the only hell fire there is!

> Stumbling in the dark towards the Light,
> Yours with love as always,
> Clare

In the June 1975 issue of the *Review* Clare further expressed:

THE DAY OF RECKONING

The day of reckoning has come, though perhaps we should use the plural tense since more lies ahead until towards the end of the century, when the new order will be more firmly established after the break-up and consequent chaos of the old which we are experiencing now, and will for some time to come. We are approaching the dissolving of the wrong and corrupt kind of materialism which is fighting hard to keep its hold over individuals, society, governments and nations alike. And every one of us, in one way or another, is involved, suffering as we are from age-long results of that materialism, its greed, its attempts to keep power, its domination, and all the manifold results which we are now seeing on every hand, and which affect almost every aspect of our personal lives. It is greed and power which brings too much luxury on the one hand, and famine on the other, which causes the earth to rebel upsetting the seasons, and so on, for if the scale tips too heavily one way, the other rises. We see this state of unablance everywhere, and are aware of it in ourselves as our plans are upset, as we are faced with the need to adapt to present conditions, as much that is unregenerate in ourselves, to our shame, rises to the surface to be understood. We are not born into this period of history by chance, for we too have debts to pay for all that we contributed in our ignorance in past lives. So it is the day of reckoning for us also, and blessed are those who perceive this, and are willing now to play their part in redeeming the causes of the present effects, by *working on themselves* so that the purposes of God may be fulfilled. Such an opportunity is open to all, and rather than lamenting all the present frustrations, we should examine our own hearts, our motives, thoughts, desires and aspirations, and ask for their cleansing and re-direction in the service of God and man.

Soon, because of the rising cost of living, petrol, railway fares and almost everything we can think of, we shall be obliged not only to live more simply and frugally, which will be very good for our health of soul, mind and body but to stay at home. But it has been said that we do not have to go anywhere, or do anything in particular, but only to be. Do you not see the spiritual opportunities now being given us in the midst of these deprivations, for becoming more still and quiet, appreciating more than ever before what we *have* got? It can be a rewarding adventure.

Then because of housing and fuel shortages, we cannot get away from one another as in the old days, where a comparative privacy meant so much to us. Young people have to live with parents; experiments in communal living are growing and not only amongst the young; the old have to leave beloved homes to receive their food and shelter with others elsewhere. And so on. All these are opportunities towards better relationships with our fellows, which bring out in us subtle forms of selfishness which have ruled us for so long. Not easy — none of it. But perhaps this is why Henry Thomas Hamblin said we are always in the right place at the right time, and when we have assimilated the lessons in self-understanding and in the acceptance they provide, we are moved on elsewhere. And this will be according to the change in our attitudes. There comes a wonderful sense of liberation when we accept and seek to understand this truth, for then indeed we know we are at home wherever we are. And having given ourselves to that underlying harmony of the universe which is evident in the intricate and marvellous world of Nature (despite what man's greed does to the Great Mother) then everything is allowed to fall naturally into place for us. No longer do we seek to manipulate life, despite all the outer appearances, but to 'let go and let God' for are we not children of His Love and wisdom, however far the prodigal sons that we are may have strayed from His ever-open Kingdom which is within us?

The day for seeking salvation for ourselves alone is over. Hence the emerging of group consciousness everywhere, not only in the multitude of private homes "where two or three are gathered together" but in countless other ways. The acceleration of separate souls being brought together to link and communicate, to invoke the Light they serve for the enlightenment and upliftment of the world, is being speeded up. And this is because the harvest is great but the labourers few, and the need is urgent. We do not necessarily have to go anywhere for this to happen, for it is under the direction of Higher Beings who seek to guide, teach and inspire us. *They need our co-operation.* And sooner or later their efforts, through us, will reach through the blindness of governments, the arts and sciences, education, medicine and all forms of technology to help man evolve nearer to his spiritual heritage. Then the causes of the present abuses and consequent suffering will be dissolved, and we shall see the beginning of God's purposes being fulfilled.

And also the days of the cloister and cave are passing. Let us never, however, depreciate the dedication of those past, present and to come, who seek through the power of prayer to enlighten our darkness. Henry Thomas Hamblin once said that if there was a sufficient number of contemplatives the world could be saved overnight from the brink of the precipice. Without contemplation how we would miss the heritage of the wisdom of the past from the saints and sages of the great religions, as we would be deprived of the comfort, challenges, refreshment and teaching, given to us by the contemplatives of our own day. Even so, they are but signposts. It has been said "thou canst not tread the Path until thou hast become the Path itself". It lies at the heart of our own experience.

This is why we have said we do not have to go anywhere or be anything in particular. One may be a business executive or a dustman, a prima donna or a housewife, famous or obscure, rich or poor, in good health or sick, but all are one in the sight of God, as all are channels in their degree when offered as such in His service. The values of the spiritual realms are different from those of this world, and happy are we when we discover them and become attuned to them.

"How beautiful are the feet of Him upon the mountains who bringeth good tidings ..." We need to ascend the mountains of the spirit to strengthen our faith which, when applied in daily life, becomes knowledge; we need the refreshment and renewal of the purer air; we need the bigger perspective that we can only see from a height; we need to communicate there with our own souls, with invisible Hosts. This is why meditation is becoming increasingly sought and practised world over, sometimes perhaps as a way of escape from a world too awful to be borne (although this is not meditation but fantasy), but chiefly because of the growing need to find the peace of the inner life and discover how to serve better in the world.

Our quiet times are essential, as the mystics have taught, if we are to play our part more intelligently, for now it is through involvement in the world that the spiritual life is to express itself. There is no evasion of responsibilities — quite the contrary, for these grow and we find ourselves becoming more active in all kinds of ways than ever, once we are released from our self-imposed prisons in which we have sought security for so long. This too is the answer to all forms of isolation and loneliness. Give yourself whole-heartedly to whatever it is that God requires of you, different for each one of us, and as has been said "the world will make a pathway to your door". Friends on your wavelength, 'who speak our language' as we say, wil inevitably gravitate to you, and this compensates for the loss of many so-called and misunderstanding friends who have deserted you since they were not yet ready for the greater understanding, for release from personal claims, and the willingness of the soul to serve. But you look back, and see how very worthwhile the pilgrimage has been.

Meanwhile, as we give ourselves more and more to the life of the Spirit while at the same time doing our best to embody it on earth, so that we seem to have our being in two worlds at once, the process of integration begins. Having glimpsed and given ourselves to the Whole, the whole of creation under the dominion of the Most High, we too become whole. As we said earlier, the underlying harmony takes over and brings us the healing of the soul which must precede the healing of the body if it is indeed true spiritual healing. (Incidentally this is why some physical ailments return after attending a Healing Service, and the immediate response of the body does not last; or the total healing may be long delayed, disappointed though we may be, tending to doubt and blame the healer. It asks much of us, if the entire attitude is to be changed and raised; if we are to be cleansed and redirected.)

So we see we have to pass through many inner processes before 'the mountains' and 'the plains' can be related to us, and we can pass freely from one to the other, from the Spirit to the flesh along the bridge of the soul. Yet bridges we are called to be, in the midst of these days of reckoning, no longer so afraid of the 'appearances' all about us since we have a foothold in eternity, and by our serenity are able to help others also towards that foothold. In all humility we fall too often back into the illusions that afflict the ordinary man, but the call of God in the soul, and a growing self-awareness brings us back, and we are established again in our own deep centre which, once we have our being there, we see is everywhere about us.

So we work, whatever our occupation or destiny, whether deprived or realising "all is taken care of", in any circumstances whatsoever, behind the scenes where we prefer to be, and where so often the children of God are found. May you be one of them, and know the sense of fulfilment, contentment and thanksgiving it brings, once we are no longer so deceived by the present appearances of the temporal all about us, distressing as they are. As we have said, they are inevitable since man is reaping as he has sown. The day will come, though perhaps not in our time, when he will sow God-given seeds upon the earth that has been purged of its evil, and open to the wind and the sun of Heaven.

Though we were not able to meet often at this time, our friendship through letters and telephone calls drew us ever closer in our hearts. I treasured with respect the many qualities which Clare embodied such as endurance, strength, courage, sincerity, integrity, empathy, vulnerability, a sense of humour and many more ... I fondly remember a particular incident relating to the latter which occurred in the summer of 1975 when Fif, Kaladin and Lalena (our two-and-a-half-year-old daughter) were visiting Clare.

We were all sitting on the lawn, partly under the shade of a tree as the sun was very hot. Lorna had been giving the children wheelbarrow rides around the garden when Kaladin approached us with a water-pistol! Moving round to face 'Auntie' Clare, he pointed the water-pistol and squirted a jet of water straight into her face. I felt embarrassed and cross with Kaladin at the time but Clare's reaction was one of laughter and she said to him, "That was most refreshing, do it again!" which he did! On many occasions over the years she was very patient with the children and loved to join in their fun and would have little conversations with them, pointing out how good they were at certain things and drawing out of them their finer qualities. She often did this with adult friends too, encouraging their strengths and pointing out their potential.

8

Shadows, Light and Release

In 1974 another collection of Clare's poems titled *Over the Rim* was published by Outpost Publications, Walton-on-Thames, Surrey. It sold out soon after it appeared. This was the first collection for some years to reach a wider public other than the privately published booklets of poems which she had been sending out to friends at Christmas. Some had appeared originally in *The Lady, The Middle Way, The Observer* and the anthology, *New Renascence.*

One in particular which shall always remain special to me was written after a visit one early autumn morning when Clare, Lorna and myself went for a walk in a large wooded area on the slopes of the Downs. Clare and I had stopped for a while beside a beautiful beech tree while Lorna wandered on a little way along a twisting pathway. After a short period of silent communication with this king of trees we continued on our way but could not find Lorna anywhere. We searched some of the paths leading in different directions and I remember at one point, after Clare and I had been searching separately, I met up with Clare and silently we turned down another path and there was Lorna! All three of us could have lost each other for hours but in a very short time we were united. None of us had been worried, instead each of us very much felt the presence of God on that autumn morning amongst the healing peace of the trees 'when we, who had been lost, were found'.

LEGEND

You came towards me through the trees
Whose coins were drifting through the windless air.
You came through the curtains of the mist
That steeped the woods in silence there.

You did not speak. What was to say?
Our footsteps were the only sound
Across the carpets of the leaves
That scattered golden from the ground.

149

The church was quiet, but there were flowers,
We gave our knees to the cold stone.
Hand invisible then raised us up
And blessed us. We were not alone.

The centuries were bridged. There was
No morrow, yesterday, today.
The silence, radiance and stillness
Drained all thought, desire and prayer away.

We rose, and smiled, one to the other turning ...
Close by, the farm, and in the shadowed byre
In straw the new-born calves, warm,
A cat asleep, in the heart of an English shire.

And all was one, within those magic moments
Of time arrested in tranquillity,
Remembering the simple words of One who said
So long ago: "The truth shall set you free."

Who came towards me through the trees?
Whence the power that gently silenced sound
Upon the morning graven on the mist
When we, who had been lost, were found?

The church mentioned in this poem is situated on a hill, near to a farm at Up Marden. Clare was very fond of the little old churches hidden away in the Sussex Downs but, of them all, Up Marden church, dating from the twelfth century, was by far her favourite. She once described it:

It is always very quiet in the white church in the hills. It is said that the present 12th century church was built on a pre-Christian site, which may account for the vibrant power of the stillness which meets me every time I enter it, so that I smile, as if coming Home. There is no village, only a farm and the manor, and it is but an old track that leads to it. It has some fragments of the finest old English glass in the country. Its proportions, as its spaciousness, are beautiful, and in their simplicity, deeply satisfying.

One Sunday afternoon I entered with a friend, and few people were already assembled — not more than half a dozen perhaps — to be followed by a young priest. My friend said: "Would you like to stay for the service?" I cried, "O no, no, no!" For I was aware of the old rituals, the chanting, the majesty and the power of the true worship still taking place there in the stillness as it was long ago, and I could not have borne what would have seemed like a travesty.

Every time I enter the purity of the white church, ageless and enduring, it cleanses me of all that is unimportant, and challenges me. It gives me recognition, assurance, strength to go on in daily life. And these words are my testimony to it. There, in the age-old peace which is power, I return my adoration and my love. But it does belong to this time. Or is it waiting to be recognised, recovered, and brought to heal the troubles of *our* time?

Not long after we first met, Clare had taken me there one sunlit afternoon and I was deeply moved by the pure and peaceful atmosphere between its crumbling walls. We sat with eyes closed on the worn wooden trestle near the altar and I was acutely aware of moving figures in blue robes, circling around us. Later, when sharing this experience with Clare, she said, "I am so glad that you have seen them for I have been aware of their presence for a long time, they belong to an order of evolved souls who inhabit a higher realm." I was so glad that I had been able to see them too as Clare had not told me of their existence previously.

Her remark did not surprise me as I knew that she was psychic and at times very aware of other beings, mostly angelic. She also told me later that day that when we had entered the grounds of the church, a group of these evolved, blue-robed beings had come out to greet us which, to Clare, signified that they knew me from long ago.

On many occasions over the years together we visited this special little church and at other times she took friends and visitors there. She always returned renewed and further inspired.

Often in her company I was aware of angelic presences. The special friendship, understanding and depth of communication we shared seemed to provide a doorway into the fourth dimension and served to make me much more conscious of the spiritual nature of life.

Her insight, intuition and visionary perception and the way she expressed her knowledge of that inner life through her writings has been compared to the writings and experiences of the Irish mystic, George William Russell, who often wrote anonymously under the initials AE. During the earlier period of Clare's life, they had met and corresponded with each other for some time. One of her treasured books was *The Candle of Vision** by AE (an autobiography

*Published by the Theosophical Publishing House, 68 Great Russell St, London.

of a mystic). She very much identified with his experiences, description of higher states of consciousness and with his visionary spirit. She deeply *knew* as AE and many others did of the reality of those higher spheres through whose open doorway she had often stepped, whilst spending time in the beauty of Nature; when writing at her desk or within the walls of an aged church. In fact she was blessed with such experiences in many ordinary everyday places too and at times when she least expected them.

Her giving indeed knew no restrictions. It was in numerous, special little ways that her giving and thoughtfulness touched me the most. During one of my stays with Clare at this time, I mentioned in conversation that I did not possess a watch. She said, "I feel sure the angels will send you one." A few days later a small package arrived from a jewellers in Chichester and, on opening it, I discovered a watch — there was no note inside! I wrote to Clare asking her to please thank the angels for me!

On another occasion we were partaking of a ploughman's lunch at a historic country pub. Having not eaten from the previous day I was very hungry and had finished my lunch before Clare was halfway through hers. She noticed my plate was empty and, taking the remaining bread from her own plate she placed it in my hand, looked into my eyes and smiled — there was no need for words. I was very moved by the simple gesture and her awareness of my need.

Whenever I stayed with Clare she saw to my every comfort as she did with all her guests and always there would be a little vase of freshly picked flowers beside my bed and a book by the lamp which contained a message which I needed to read. Through her, I often found the answers to unuttered questions which resided in the domain of my heart.

Her love of truth and beauty, her understanding and her relationship with God deeply inspired me just as much as did her sharing of her very human qualities and struggles. In one way she was just as full of fears, inner restlessness, anxieties and battles with her self-will as is anyone else, yet in another way she was very God-inspired, unique and very much a mystic with saint-like qualities which made her stand apart from a crowd. Her being contained many shadows as well as much light. She often felt a deep sadness when readers of the *Review* placed her on a pedestal and she longed more than anything to be loved and fully accepted for *all* of herself: the very human Clare with her struggles and fears as well as the divinely inspired Clare with her wisdom and enlightened vision.

In 1976, through requests from many of her readers, another poem book appeared called *Memories of Eden*, published by the Mitre Press and now out of print. Some of these verses had previously appeared in *A Stranger Here* (1942), *Far from Home* (1944), the recent *Over the Rim* as well as the Christmas booklets; other poems were new ones. Here is one of the many which spoke of her search for the divine:

INSIGHT

Here, I am awake.
A wind from the beyond has shaken sleep from my eyes.
Stretched and still, I am clear skies
That rain down light upon the world we know
I see the truth of things, as in an afterglow.
Outlines sharp and clear — all that is false and poor
Dissolve in shadow and swiftly are no more,
Leaving the essential, in majesty and grace.
My Lord Invisible, Thou fillest every place
With diamond Light!

Peace brims my heart.
Soon or late, the heart of every man will fill
With this sweet clarity the heavens distill,
Wherein is insight, calm, and charity,
The wisdom of the truth that sets us free.
Over the dreaming world I meditate this Light
To wake some soul this night, or another night
Into the Will of God, so vast, so deep,
Who in His Perfect Love doth each one keep.

The beauty of her poetry, her wide vision and inner clarity certainly was instrumental in awakening many people to a deeper and not so clouded perception of the spiritual nature of life. But often she would say, "There are parts of me that cannot live up to what I write about and I know them only too well." Not only was she aware of those higher, more evolved parts of her nature which were very in tune with the inifinite but she was equally aware of the lower parts of her nature; her possessive and selfish traits; her demanding self-will which, in the past, had made intimate relationships with lovers quite stormy and also resulted in the loss of a few friendships of either sex; her lack of faith through times of darkness and struggle; her deep need for a close companion which would rise and overwhelm her partner and drive him or her further away. She found it very easy to accept weaknesses of character and the unevolved, unintergrated parts of others but found it extremely difficult to accept similar parts in herself. I not only loved the finer qualities which flowed inspiringly through her in so many ways but I loved even more those very unintegrated parts because they made her so human, just like anyone else. Indeed the depth of understanding and the help she was to others in her personal life as well as through her writings would not have been so meaningful and genuine if it had not been born out of her own conflicts and difficulties.

In June 1978 I received from Clare:

Dear Brian,

There is so much we do not understand at this time when some of us seem beset by fog, frustration, disappointments, and much that puzzles us, while others go forward into change for the better. I too seem to have come to a full stop and carry on more or less mechanically, doing only what I am obliged to do, unable to read or concentrate, and yet none of it is physical, so we must be attacked on the etheric levels. I scarcely know what I am doing most of the time. We are too vulnerable, though I do practise invoking the enclosing sphere of Light.

I too know those clouds of depression and almost despair at times, as if my life is in ruins, though we know the phoenix will rise from the ashes. We seem to have touched rock bottom and yet there is still more. But on another and higher plane we know much is happening in the soul, and in that is more and more of our trust, awaiting more and more surrender. There are so many resistances that we are not aware of.

I am almost chain-smoking now, which doesn't help, but seem unable to stop. Yet my work gets done, somehow, which is marvellous. My breathing is affected and I stagger in my walk, but feel it isn't entirely due to the smoking.

Well, my dear, though we seem so alone in what we are passing through, deliverance could come suddenly, and may be at our very doors. After all, even Christ felt forsaken in Gethsamene, and if we follow Him then every step of the way must be trodden, and all the more wonderful will be the resurrection.

Is all that is important taken care of? We know it is despite the quite alarming appearances and the restrictions of the personality. In that is our trust, all we have now, but all have to come to it, sooner, and the more we climb the harder the going, as the saints have known.

Forgive such a letter, but it may be comfort to you to know you are not alone on this spiritual pilgrimage.

Hand in hand with you over the stony ground.

Ever love
Clare

1978 also saw the publishing of *Without Going out of the Door* by the Research Publishing Company. This was a collection of Clare's essays, containing the quintessence of her thinking, which had appeared over the years in the *Review*. In the foreword, Sir George Trevelyan drew attention to how beautifully and wisely the essays were written, the help they gave to many in dark and disturbing times, and how they encouraged the holding on to the vision of the truth. Published by the request of many readers of the magazine it was well received and much appreciated.

But, despite the increased recognition of her worth, Clare was continuing to experience a lot of inner tension and turmoil. Only close friends knew how she truly felt. To the many visitors to Bosham House and to the readers of the *Review*, she continued to be looked up to for her depth of wisdom and understanding.

She was feeling beaten to her knees and that she could do nothing about it; yet, at the same time, for her age (eighty-two) she was achieving much more than she realized. She was still able to express herself beautifully through her writings, as she did in this article written around this time:

A BOWL OF WILD FLOWERS

They are before me, eloquent, poised in stillness, clear in colour and perfect in grace. What a privilege it is to look upon them! How dare I attempt to write about them, since they themselves are the perfect testimony of the ideal life? I have heard it said that flowers should not be taken into rooms, for their proper place is in the garden, the meadow and the wood. Recently a friend said that every time he plucks a flower he feels he is taking life. There is so much to be said for both points of view that I am almost apologetic when gathering them. For to my care in arranging them, and with a certain homage, they offer indifference. They are immune from human reactions. They live in a world of their own, in their own paradise. Paradise! Again it is said that of all the kingdoms, human, animal, vegetable and mineral, the flower kingdom was the least involved in the Fall, and to this day remains nearest therefore to the Heart of God. Is this why, when giving ourselves to them in meditation, so that we are identified with their consciousness, we are at times stirred almost beyond bearing? The return to our normal selves, the life that we know, and the world as man has made it, is a shock. O so wide the gap between this beauty, this integrity, this flame-like peace; completion and fulfilment, and our drab, complex and muddled lives! They live, eternally in the Light, while we still grope in the shadows. They are at Home, while we are still in the Far Country.

They toil not, neither do they spin. They unfold their little miracles, and in a few days wilt and die. Without water they shrivel before their time. A heedless foot can crush them. Fragile and fugitive, they are yet so strong that they mutiply in their thousands in an untended meadow or woodland glade. What is the secret of their power? Gazing upon them, why are we aware of a more intense life than we have ever known ourselves?

Because the same intense life beats somewhere strongly within us; because we have been, and still can be, part of their beauty, integrity, fulfilment and joy. We cannot recognise that which we have never known.

The gate of Paradise has never been shut, although the Flaming Sword still forbids the entrance of anything that is not of the paradisical nature. Yet sweet and over-powering influences, strong with the verity of eternity, are constantly flowing through. O my friends, we shall never discover the way in books, which at best are only half-alive and fragmentary, and the statements in them blurred by the limited and misshapen minds through which the truth endeavours to pass. The Light is in some of them, reflections caught by the artists and saints, and according to whether it shines clear or dim, the memory of the soul is stirred as we read.

But in the bowl of wild flowers, plucked from a common hedgerow, the Light blazes, the Word is spoken in ringing tones, and radiant vistas are opening before our wondering eyes. Through this gate we re-enter Paradise.

And what shall we bring back with us: we may be so profoundly moved that we are compelled, sooner or later, to change our way of life entirely, being unable any longer to live in terms of compromise, evasion and superficial content. If we are to have peace of mind henceforth, we may have to rise up out of our weakness and challenge all that we know to be dishonest, ugly, corrupt, mean or unkind, all that is not in true alignment with the ideal of life.

Yes, the flowers bring us not only beauty, joy and peace. They may bring illumination. They may bring a vivid *awakening*.

I am glad I brought them into my room, for the Master was in the midst of them.

In another letter in February 1979 Clare wrote:

Dear Brian,

Indeed we are "being cleansed and purified as never before that we may be more worthy channels for fuller service to others in the future". But I cannot *feel* anything and seemed blocked. The energy is there but cannot get out, and no guidance comes. It's more and more of an effort to write a letter. One cannot but continue to release everything to the Lord. All must be well for us all — the soul knows this and rejoices.

Though I have known misery and despair again, more than ever scarcely knowing what I am doing, very forgetful and making mistakes in my work. And I simply can't stop smoking which is making me so breathless and tending to fall about, though there may be other causes of course. Some very profound process is taking place within us, dear Brian, and we must let it, letting go and letting God.

Every morning I wonder how I'm going to get through the day but it is wonderful how everything is taken care of. It will be still more wonderful when I can think and feel again, and recover some interest. This ignorant little personality still feels the waters going over her head, and the inertia increases. One cannot help crying at times "Lord, how long?"

I know the lower self fights to the last ditch, and the last struggling steps up the mountain to get a higher and wider view are the hardest. Meanwhile we know the purifying process goes on, and that it is all really an answer to prayer.

I shall be grateful for your prayers for my breathing is terrible now. The pressure from all sides is acute. You certainly have mine.

Ever love from
Clare

I was going through a personal crisis in my own life at the time with imminent changes on the horizon as a result of the breakdown of my marriage. I didn't realize at the time that the outcome of the transitional period which I was going through would soon bring Clare and I even closer.

Within these pages I have only included a few of the many letters which Clare wrote me over the years. Letters of inspiration and encouragement; of despair and struggle; of support and comfort. Every single one, no matter what their content, were very dear to me.

Dick Batstone, another friend from Clare's days when she was closely associated with the Sri Aurobindo group in London, recalls the warmth of personal interest and concern which she had for people. When they were in correspondence she once wrote:

Dear Dick,

Surely, in the parable, the ploughman having set his hand to the plough, should *not* look back but just persevere, thereby acquiring 'skill in action', learning steadfastness and patience, and he is better grounded in life itself than the too-ambitious man, however spiritual his ideals may be? We cannot run before we walk. Often, Dick, there are years of this inertia, so well explained in *The Cloud of Unknowing* which may be because one is in a cleft stick, and uncertain, or maybe also because much is happening in the soul, but hidden from us. And do remember, that even what we imagine to be our mistakes are not really so, but part of our experience and growth, and most wonderfully 'worked in' by the Divine. I have found this profoundly true, and it is a great comfort. We can but do our best, and the Lord knows the heart, ignoring all our whims and fancies and doubts which we, in our ignorance and narrow view, think so important!

But always in uncertainty, is it not better to restrain the ignorant active mind as much as one can, and cultivate the surrender, the inner quiet ...

Through the many thousands of letters of guidance, comfort and encouragement which Clare wrote to her readers and friends, many were helped in understanding how to use their difficulties as stepping stones to becoming more wise, integrated and whole. Her warmth and care certainly showed itself in her lines and in all her personal contacts but she herself needed to be listened to in the restless and difficult period she was now experiencing. Underneath the surface there was a battle raging within her which, at the best of times, prevented her from reaching that greater depth of inner quiet which she so much longed for.

The turbulent waters through which she was passing and the feelings of helplessness were very evident in her editorial in the August 1979 issue of the *Review*. This particular article and what Clare shared within its lines became one of the most popular that she ever wrote:

THE TIDE

It is coming in with increasing rapidity, sweeping away all the debris on our shores, all our former concepts, ideas, beliefs, attachments and, if only we can understand the promise it holds, the habits perhaps of a lifetime. We are being cleansed and purified as never before, that we may be more worthy channels for what lies ahead for us in service to others. And those of us who have this knowledge will be needed to help others understand when the waters go over their heads in days to come. We shall reach out hands to those who could so easily drown under the waves of fear, anxiety, depression, despair. Even we ourselves at the present time can sink into inertia, indifference and a feeling of helplessness or ride the waves with courage and hope.

For there is no doubt that just as the whole world is changing now that the old order of things is breaking down to release the beginnings of the new, so we ourselves are changing. We are obliged to recognise it. There is no more security in all the aspects of our lives, no more security in the familiar and the comfortable, either physically, mentally, emotionally or the kind of spirituality that has served us in the past. Under this tide of higher vibrations and cosmic energies, the ground is going from under our feet. There are new shores ahead, but only this tide can carry us to them.

Because of all this, we may no longer know who or where we are. Timelessness from another dimension is penetrating the time we know. Something far bigger and more meaningful is taking over, or seeking to do so, and we must let it. For it will bring harmony into the discords, order out of muddle, Divine adjustments in our affairs and circumstances, an awareness of effortlessness in place of effort as we fulfill the responsibiities of the average day. This happens when we let the tide carry us towards the new understanding, the expansion of consciousness that releases us from all our past limitations.

New wine is not poured into old bottles. We have to let go of everything that we may be re-filled and fulfilled as we never thought possible. Depth upon depth may be revealed to us, the fruit of our conditioning. We observe calmly and accept it all, for only then can we understand what it means to be a human being, and become filled with compassion for ignorant mankind who makes so much of his own suffering. Perhaps this is why Jesus the Christ descended into hell, to cleanse those dark realms.

Since all life is one what is happening to us personally is happening to our world in its travail towards re-birth which may not happen until the next century or beyond. But whoever we are, sick or well, normal or handicapped, famous or obscure, we can enter into it by enduring with fortitude our own suffering which can be transcended once we have this deeper and wider understanding.

But we simply must *let go* of all the claims of the little self, and, as your Editor knows so well, it takes time. But just as the angels are patient with us, so we must learn to be patient, and above all, trust a Love and Wisdom that, according to our obedience, is taking over. This Love and Wisdom is at work in our world, confirmed by the multitude of groups dedicated to service of God and man, by more caring and sharing in various ways, by the examples of the young who are already participating in this new consciousness, the increasing interest in meditation, the decline of support of orthodox religion until it breaks free from dogma and doctrine and provides the living Bread instead of stones, as a few enlightened priests here and there are already doing.

Riding the waves which support us in a wonderful way, we reject the bewilderment and fears of the little self which so easily projects its blame upon our circumstances, what the world at the present time is doing to us, or depriving us of. *All that must go.*

Until we begin to make it, we have no idea of what is required of us when we surrender ourselves to God. Just as well. A little at a time. That is all that is expected of us. Gradually we learn as we go along. That sea ahead of us, of expanding consciousness which is not acquired from books necessarily, will give to us in a secret manner all we need to know. It will feed and sustain all the levels of the being.

When we have given ourselves to Christ, the inner Lord, how do we react? For He still walks the waters and with lifted hands says "Peace, be still". Once we recognise this, we carry that deep inner peace through all hazards, all trials, all perils, all problems, and stormy waters no longer bring any fear to us.

An impossible ideal? No. It is open to every one of us, the hidden gateway to eternal life here and now. Why postpone the opportunity? Our little barque may be frail and small, but it can ride the waves, and beyond them there are harbours from whence we shall bring back Heavenly treasure to share with others, as we move with new understanding through our troubled worlds. For some of us it is our privilege and our responsibility. Let go and let God. He waits out there on the incoming tide.

Though there were periods of inspiration and calm, Clare continued to be involved in a war within herself. Early in 1980 she revealed more of her personal anguish:

Dear Brian,

I have been very much aware of what you have been passing through and can echo your own words about our resistances being broken down and burnt out, and how painful is the fire! It's also as if new wine is being pressed out of us, so acute is the pressure. I've never felt more terrible in my life and feel worse every day. But it is darkest before the dawn, and a new life awaits us both, though where and how we do not know, for I too live from moment to moment.

For a long time now I have lost interest in everything, and now my work seems even more affected. I am ashamed of being so negative about everything, and so self-centred.

It is like being on a battlefield between the dark forces and the Light, and one feels half strangled in between.

O Brian, how far one seems to have to go down in making a total commitment to God! I haven't reached the bottom yet by any means, but am aware of increasing Light upon all that has to be surrendered. It isn't a pleasant sight but one has to look at it calmly.

We shall come through together, dear Brian, for I feel changes imminent, unfit as I am to cope with them.

May the Divine Harmony take over the whole of our lives.

Meanwhile ever love

Clare

In the summer of 1980 my wife and I separated and I went to America for three months to sort myself out before starting to build a new life. I had no idea at the time what I was going to do or where I was going to live upon my return to England.

Not long before I left Clare shared with me her anxieties and fears about not being able to continue the editorship of the *Review* and of what would happen to her. She asked me in a letter if I would consider becoming the new editor. Because of all my own struggles and personal difficulties at the time I felt I could not accept such a big responsibility. I needed time to be alone and integrate all that was happening inside of me with such a major change in my life.

We continued to keep in touch while I was overseas. A few weeks before I was to return I wrote to Clare asking her if she would contact a few of our mutual friends in the west Sussex area about finding a place to live for me. Within weeks I was offered a bungalow by the sea at West Wittering, about ten miles from Bosham House. In the autumn of 1980, upon my return, I moved into my new place of residence on agreement with the owner that it would be only temporary. Soon after settling there I took up a career in psychiatric nursing, helped by a reference from Clare.

During the next few months Clare visited me often and I cycled over to Bosham House to spend a night. Lorna, whose health had rapidly deteriorated, had now moved to a nursing home in Chichester and Clare was sharing her house with Richard Passey, a violin restorer from Wales whom she employed as a driver and companion. Richard had been a reader of the *Review* for many years and they both shared similar interests. We had many an enjoyable evening together sharing our deepest thoughts and feelings.

Clare was still feeling very unsure as to what was going to happen to her as, in her present mental state and with the increasing limitations of her age, everything was getting too much for her. Still she battled on, editing the magazine, answering many letters daily, receiving a stream of visitors and going to conferences, meetings and regular visits to friends.

Despite her troubled feelings, she put on a brave face and managed, by the grace of God, to carry on. She was finding it extremely difficult to accept the limitations of her age. For some time now she had not been able to go on her much-loved walks across the Downs because of lack of strength and breathlessness; yet part of her still felt young at heart. Her struggles to accept her limitations added to the anxiety and frustration she was already experiencing. It saddened her greatly that she had hardly any inspiration or creative upsurge to write.

Yet, from out of the depths of her despair and her increasing self-criticism, she still wrote inspiringly, as is evident in this article in the *Review* in December of that year.

CHRIST IN YOU

He is born of Virgin consciousness, purified of all impediments, wherein is the recovered innocence of a little child, born in all humility, sometimes when all else has been taken from us, that we may be set free from all illusion and ignorance. He is born in a secret place, because there is no room in the inn of materialism. He is not recognised by the world, but only by the angelic hosts, the wise men who have heard about Him from afar, the simple shepherds, all of whom pay Him homage as the Son of God.

He was let down from Heaven, the Source of Divinity, by His own choice, sacrificing the radiance, the beauty, the inexpressible joy of the Higher Realms that He might bring love to earth, filling the hearts of those who were prepared to accept it and to follow Him with all the similar sacrifices it might involve.

As we follow the Star, we are led through deserts, jungles and the wilderness, and like Him, it may seem we have nowhere to lay our heads. We are called to be steadfast, patient, enduring, and to continue in faith where we cannot see. This is the beginning of the inward service to God and man, and it may or may not express itself outwardly. The Star leads us to find and allow to be expressed through our purpose in life, different for each one as it was for the disciples. As we approach the manger, and kneel with the beasts, not only do we know we are in a holy place, but we know that all that lives is holy. Whatever may be happening to us outwardly, understanding, peace and joy flood the soul. All our problems, and they may be mutiple, fall away, for they no longer seem of any importance; fear and anxiety are replaced by hope and an ever-growing trust; the personality is transcended for we have one foot in Heaven.

We see in the helpless tiny Babe a replica of ourselves, as God sees us, and know that indeed we are made in the image of God. We do not know what lies ahead of us, any more than Jesus did (or did He?) but it does not matter any more, for we know the angels will be with us to all eternity and treasure from Heaven will be given to us so long as we keep in touch with the Higher consciousness. This is of the utmost importance, for by straying from it we are caught up again in the illusions and ignorance of the world, betrayed by its glamour, falling into temptation, and behaving like the average man.

The soul is always obedient, and with infinite patience awaits the cooperation of the personality which was incarnated to learn through experience. And all too often we prolong the pain of it through wilfulness, wanting our own way. How foolish, and for so long, can we be! And yet it has great value, for we find we can forgive anyone and everyone as we become more reduced, more aware of the folly of human nature. The Love of God for all humanity streams through us, to friends and enemies alike, across the whole world, racked by turmoil and wars, by earthquakes, floods, all the inequality resulting in the contrasts of riches and acute poverty. Then we are indeed following in the footsteps of Jesus the Christ and peace returns to the heart.

As we allow the God-guided soul to take over, we have an increasing distaste for the things that men of the world consider desirable; they have been outgrown, and fall away naturally, making room for the things of good report, which bring more enduring happiness. Happiness? By a strong paradox, while the personality may continue unhappy, at the deep centre there is joy, the joy that we know in the stable, the joy that is the ultimate heritage of all mankind, and which, through our dedication we are helping to bring to pass, though we may not see it during the life of the body.

But we have to leave the stable, and return to the world, and as far as possible, take the glad tidings. Because our dedication still falls short, this can be very difficult, for there is such an acute contrast between what came to us before the manger and the life of the world. There, everything was seen as holy, but back in the everyday all may seem tawdry and vulgar, the ambitions of men, resulting in so much competition, so stupid, the ignorance like the darkness of a prison in which so many spend their lives. This is where we must invoke again the compassion, the humility, the simplicity, the obedience, and allow the Christ-consciousness to see through our eyes, and the divine purpose to be expressed through us.

At this time in history when there seems to be a battle between the forces of darkness and the Light, in which we may be caught up, this is not easy, and we may find ourselves in an impasse.

This may feel like climbing a mountain, weary and with bleeding feet, but it takes us up towards the radiance of the sun, and gives a perspective we can never achieve on the plains.

There may be also an inner loneliness, despite a multitude of friends, the loneliness that many of the mystics knew, and Jesus Himself when deserted by His friends, in Gethsemane, on the way to the Cross, and during His crucifixion. But even if we can feel the presence of the angels with us, this is infinitely more satisfying than the companionship of earthly friends, and it is this which those confined to their rooms or beds know, and which may be sensed by those who visit them.

Let us make more room for the wise and beautiful Will of God, who sent His Messenger as a bridge between earth and Heaven at Christmas and then what has returned to becoming an almost pagan festival will be transformed to a hymn of praise and thanksgiving. At this beautiful season of goodwill, this does not mean withdrawal or lack of participation, but keeping a balance between what belongs to man and what belongs to God.

Another collection of Clare's editorials, articles and poems, *Mystic of Nature*, was published in 1980 by Skilton & Shaw. Martin Israel in the foreword spoke of her writings bringing a balm to the soul and refreshment to those who are weary and depressed; "they all bear the stamp of one who is blessed with a mystical vision of the unity of all things in God". Again this new volume was well received.

At the beginning of 1981 I had to leave my seaside home and, with no other home evident on the horizon, Clare said, "You must come here." With the help of friends I moved into Bosham House with Clare and Richard. And so began a new chapter in my life and also in Clare's as I began assisting her in the work of the magazine as well as attending to my duties at the hospital. The help I was able to give in sharing some of the responsibilities of the magazine and the household chores relieved Clare's anxieties to a degree. Now that she had more help she felt she could continue her editorship of the *Review*; this lessened the urgency of finding a new editor, and also of Clare having to look for a new home.

In the spring of 1981 Richard returned to his home in Wales. In the meantime Clare had offered a room in Bosham House to another friend, Robert How, who was looking for somewhere to live.

Robert and I took it in turns to see to the household chores and cook the evening meal for all of us. Robert had a car and used to take Clare out whenever he could. Clare found it very difficult to remain in the house for any length of time. She was much happier when she was out and about; calling in on friends; going to a healing meeting; attending the Sunday morning Quaker service and other gatherings of like-minded souls interested in spiritual matters. She had a great need to be with people and if she could not get out to see and mingle with others then she regularly invited friends to tea or to have dinner with us at home.

She also joined the Bahá'i faith and enjoyed being a part of their fireside circles. Her main reason for doing this was that she liked the Bahá'i's she met very much, Robert was a Bahá'i too, and she felt at home at their informal gatherings. In her heart she did not like totally to belong to any one religion as she always called herself a universalist, recognising the One Source from which all religions and different ways spring.

Robert had a natural gift for acting and playing the fool and his lively, outgoing spirit used to have both Clare and me in fits of laughter. It always made me very happy to see her laugh and enjoy herself so much. When we had friends round for dinner she particularly loved playing charades and, though she was eighty-four years old, she participated fully in such active evenings.

During the times when my children, Kaladin, Lalena and Sasha (my youngest daughter) came to join me at Bosham House on their holidays Clare always made them feel very welcome and was very accepting of their lively and adventuring spirits. She loved to talk to them and expressed her gratitude when my son Kaladin filled the log basket or coal skuttle and was deeply touched when the girls returned from the garden clutching bunches of wild flowers for her. She also insisted on doing the mountain of washing-up after we all had dinner and I was busy putting the children to bed.

She was always very eager to join what we were doing and was most surprised when she won at card games which we all played quite often when the children were with me. Her fun-loving and child-like spontaneity was very evident at such times.

Her most constant companion in the house was her cat Gilly-Puss who had been with her for years and used to follow her from room to room and around the garden. Whenever Clare was at home,

Gilly-Puss was always nearby. Gilly Puss always slept at the foot of Clare's bed and often Clare would remark how startled she was in the middle of the night when Gilly-Puss, after a late-night prowl in the garden, leapt from the windowsill in her attic bedroom, landing with a great thump on her bed! Strangely enough, exactly a month after Clare died, Gilly-Puss died too. She was killed by a car on the main road, a place where she never ventured usually. I am sure she went looking for Clare.

Up on the side of the Downs in a beech wood, the one which she mentioned in her poem 'Legend', was a very large tree of which Clare was very fond. In previous years when she was able to walk considerable distances without becoming breathless she would often spend time sitting against this king of trees in silent communication. During the summer of 1981 when the children were with us I decided to take her to visit her old and very special friend. The upward track to this tree is quite irregular and rises very steeply. Clinging to my arm for support she was determined to sit by her tree again. We had to stop often because the effort needed to climb the upward path made her breathing very laboured, but with courage and her deep belief that God would give her the strength to accomplish her task, she got there.

I shall never forget the smile that spread across her lips on seeing her favourite tree in front of her again. She went up and threw her arms around it and I felt the tree embrace her with branches unseen. She spent a little while in silent conversation with her special friend and somehow it seemed as if a healing peace spread through the tree into her body and mind bringing rest and upliftment.

She was also delighted to see Lalena and Sasha skip and play underneath its welcoming branches and quite amazed, on looking up, to find Kaladin waving at her from a vantage point in its uppermost branches!

Being a lover of trees and a mystic of nature for a great part of her life, here in the woods on this cloudless summer's day she felt truly at home.

Even though she had a multitude of friends and each of her days were very full, keeping up with her magazine work and correspondence which brought her fulfilment and meaning, deep inside she felt very isolated at times. I recall how effectively she once described her loneliness in an earlier poem.

LAMENT OF A LONELY LADY

I brought in boughs and flowers for Christmas
But no-one came.
I hung a bunch of holly on the doorpost
With red ribbons threaded through
But no-one knocked.
I hung the little angels from the lamp.
The multitude of cards on all the shelves
Were like the wings of jewelled birds alight.
The fire burned brightly on the hearth every day
But no-one saw.

I looked at the reflection in the mirror
And said to her:
One who bears your title and your name
Is known the world over
And, it seems, is greatly, sweetly loved,
But does no-one love her for herself alone?
The far-off voices come not near.
Now why is this?

There was no reply. I left my house
And walked down to the water
Where noonday sun was silvering the sea
And shelduck crooning softly
And tall reeds whispering in the wind.
And beauty could not reach my isolated heart.
Now why was this?

Back in my quiet and gracious house
I stared through the window to the garden
And I cried:
"Come, someone, break down the door!
Find the palace of the sleeping beauty!
Come in light, in truth, in power
And cleave this paralysis upon the soul
That shuts me in!"

And it seemed it was said:
"And yet, and yet
If it be the lonely sorrow of the world
Past, present or to come
That she carries in her heart,
Ah, then, she can bear it, for who knows

If here is not the womb of life to come
Sacred for a world that is to be?
Sacred for a world in anguish still?"
The reflection in the mirror smiled.
The lips moved and murmured:
'So be it, Lord, according to Thy Will.'

And then she remembered
New life is born in silence
And in isolation and must be accepted.
And she also knew
That to the boughs and flowers of Christmas
Someone had come
And the heart's barred door (for fear of further pain)
Had opened to let Someone in
Though then she knew it not.
He had warmed His hands by the fire
And blessed everyone of those greeting cards
That were tributes unto Him and not to her.

And she was ashamed,
Who had been so foolish and cast down
Who should have magnified her Lord,
Only at the time she could not,
Failing in understanding.

TAIL PIECE

The sunshine was pouring through the windows
When I came back to my house from the city.
Everything was still.
There was a stillness in the winter jasmine
Opening its tiny yellow flowers on the table
In the midst of green leaves.
There was stillness in the swift flight
Of the yellow tit to the bird table.
Tables, chairs, cushions and pictures
Were held in this dynamic stillness.
And it was said:

'I have never left you but have been with you
Since the foundation of the world,
And my Name is Love.
I am here, informing these flowers,
These birds, in the wood and the texture,

In the very walls that never hem you in,
In the sunlight and the very air.
Draw upon my Life in every breath
And know My Presence
In the earthquake, in the whirlwind and the fire,
For I am purifying and setting free
The instrument of My Peace that you are.'

In the midst of the tensions, anxieties and fears there emanated from Clare a special peace and wisdom which was felt by many. Even when she felt completely identified with these conflicting traits of her personality, still a bright light shone within the lamp of her being which touched with warmth and love the receptive hearts of those who happened to be in her company. Even when she was feeling at her worst she continued to be supportive to others whose troubles seemed greater than her own. A greatness in her shone forth despite her personal unrest and inner conflict.

One of Clare's greatest worries was her constant smoking. She had smoked cigarettes since her late teens and, although she had tried to give them up on many occasions, particularly in recent years, she was not able to stop. Her inability to do this made her even more distressed and more anxious which resulted in her smoking even more. I did encourage her to try to smoke less because of the harmful effect that it was having on her breathing. But, on the other hand, her smoking to relieve tensions made her very human and friends felt even closer to her because of it. Because of the love and warmth that flowed from her, it seemed to matter little whether she smoked or not. I know many non-smokers but none of them possess the special qualities and depth of understanding that were so evident in Clare.

Before she began her busy day she would clear out the fireplace and set the fire ready to be lit later that evening. I knew how much it meant to her to continue doing this despite her failing strength, so I never intervened. She also loved to make the afternoon tea, preparing the tray with the china cups, buttering scones and cutting cakes for visitors. It was very much a daily ritual which she much enjoyed. When Clare made the tea, something about the quiet simplicity of the ceremony, her humility and the feeling in which she served it to others was special. The way in which she did it spoke of the art of the tea ceremony, the traditional art of Japan which has evolved over the centuries as a way to self-understanding and as a means of practising true hospitality.*

Clare's favourite tea was a mixture of Twinings Nectar and Earl Grey in equal quantities; she would add a few generous pinches of herb comfrey and half a teaspoonful of maté to every spoonful of the mixed tea. Many visitors to Bosham House found this combination most refreshing and inquired about the recipe.

I have many fond memories of special and very enjoyable times we spent together. We often went to Chichester Festival Theatre to see a play or listen to the music of such composers as Mendelssohn, Debussy, Rossini, Delius, Barber, Handel, Tchaikovsky, Ravel, Beethoven, Mozart or Haydn. One of the highlights of our year was when, during the two-week annual festivities in Chichester each July, we made our way to Chichester Cathedral to see and listen to the Academy of St Martin-in-the-Fields|playing some of our favourite composers in the beautiful setting of the cathedral, lit entirely by over two thousand candles. During this performance we both experienced an ascent into a much higher state of consciousness and, on returning home, Clare would remark that she felt she had walked in the Garden of Eden. Such inspiring times provided much nourishment for Clare's soul.

Clare derived much delight when we attended a Shakespeare play out in the open within the walls of Arundel Castle. This event took place in the last week of August each year during the Arundel Festival. We took cushions to place on the hard wooden seats and a blanket to protect us from the cold evening air and, sipping mulled wine, while the moon was rising high above the battelements, we thoroughly enjoyed the performance. At other times on a summer evening we also went to the open-air plays performed in the peaceful setting and beauty of the grounds of West Dean College.

There were also times when we would drive down to the quayside at Old Bosham Harbour at midnight and stand, arm in arm, entranced by the incredible beauty of the full moon shining silver on the snow-white wings of the swans. Upon returning from such midnight adventures and just before retiring to our bedrooms Clare often amused me by saying, "Brian, I know you will understand when I say that tonight I am going to bed with you!" I knew

Zen in the Art of the Tea Ceremony by Horst Hammitzsch, Element Books, The Old Brewery, Tisbury, Wiltshire.

that she meant our souls would co-habit the same region of beauty and sacred peace.

Late one summer's night under the black canopy of the sky, lit by a full moon, we both were very conscious of the 'flow' of life. Sitting on a bench in the garden, our hearts open wide, we were transported to higher realms. There was no this or that, no communication through words — just the luminous light of the moon, a shining pearl in the gown of heaven high above us. A deep silence pervaded every atom within and without us. We both knew and felt, without having to say anything, that we were experiencing the 'flow of heaven'. It seemed that at any moment an angel clothed in white light was about to appear beside us in the garden. Close by the scent of the white roses filled the air, their satin petals forming a chalice to hold the sacred dew.

Often when I was with Clare we both experienced the unity of all life, a divine essence, a 'flow', a place not of this world yet found in this world, that resides closer to us than breathing. That night in the garden, as in other unexpected moments, we experienced it. In Clare's company in fleeting moments of heightened perception I was deeply aware of a peace sublime, a freedom and a deep, deep, joy, not of this world ...

I remember one evening I had decided to go to a concert by Shusha, a folk singer from Persia, of whose songs of freedom and love I was very fond. Thinking that the concert not only was too late but also unsuitable for Clare, I tried to discourage her not to go but she insisted that she would like to. So with another friend, the three of us ventured out into the night to the venue where the concert was being held. I remember thinking that Clare would feel uncomfortable in the company of young people only. How wrong I was! Not only were there people of all ages present but Clare was deeply touched by Shusha's beautiful voice and sincerity and, sitting round a table drinking wine, listening to the wisdom in the words of her songs, Clare's elfin face shone with a glowing light. She often repeated to friends on many different occasions afterwards how much she enjoyed that evening.

There were times when, sitting around the dancing flames of the fire, Clare would talk about her past, her painful experiences, the people she knew and her fears. She spoke of the difficulties there had been in the relationships she had with different men in her life and of the joy too. She remembered with an endearing fondness how encouraging and supporting special friends had been in troubled periods of her life; Brother Mandus, the well-known healer; Ronald Beesley a spiritual and psycho-healer; John Moreton, a mystic and painter; John Blofield, writer of books on Buddhism and Winifred Rushforth, a psychologist, were a few who stood out amongst the many.

Because of her age, her physical and mental abilities were noticeable lessening and her fears of not being able to continue with the editorship of the *Review* grew. Her memory deteriorated considerably and she found it very hard to come to terms with what was happening to her. She rarely wrote new editorials in the final years of her life but would use reprints of earlier ones. Despite her anguish at what was happening she continued bravely to keep up a front to visitors but those closer to her could see now how rapidly the ageing process was catching up on her. Nevertheless, she continued to be creative and extremely active for her years. Whenever she could Clare loved to join local 'sacred dance' groups. These dances originally come from the ancient, traditional dances of many countries and are a wordless form of prayer, a sacred dialogue with God expressed in the form of movement of the dance. Through participating in such dances, which can have a very uplifting and therapeutic effect, one can become more conscious of the inner journey — the journey of the searching soul seeking the purpose and meaning of life and leading one into a greater awareness of the one source at the heart of all. A meditation in movement.

Though at eighty-five years of age she was not able to participate in the more energetic dances she did dance all the ones she possibly could. Often upon returning from these events her heart would be bubbling with enthusiasm and joy as she felt she had danced with God. She also spoke of ancient memories of having taken part in such prayerful dances, long, long ago.

Her final years were a mixture of fears and joy. At times she experienced being lifted into a higher state of consciousness where she walked hand in hand with God, the lifelong needs of her soul fulfilled. At other times she felt lost in a stormy sea full of the anxious and fearful waves of thought that arose from those ignorant and resistent parts of her personality. Times of shadow and times of light. Times of sorrow and times of joy.

When she felt at her worst and longing to be released from her inner turmoil she sought refuge and understanding in my arms and used to cry out, "O Brian, what shall become of me!" Such tender, evocative moments I shall always remember. Holding her small, wiry frame within my arms, our souls in silent communication, a greater love gently embraced us both.

Yet, despite her own troubles, she always had time to listen to mine. The vase of freshly picked flowers would mysteriously appear on my bedside table or the little treat, some little item of food which she knew I particularly liked, would be placed in my hand. Her love and kindness to me and also to many others continued to have no boundaries.

Early in February 1983 while I was away for a few days in Bath I returned to find the house empty and a note left by Robert that Clare had been admitted to hospital with difficulties with breathing and heart. Intuitively I knew this was the end and so began five weeks of daily visits to the hospital. After extensive tests the doctors discovered she had cancer of the pancreas and it was just a matter of time.

I was besieged by letters and telephone calls from a host of friends. The number of visitors to her bedside at the hospital grew day by day until I had, on Clare's request, to ask people not to visit her, only those very close friends.

I took on the full responsibility of the editorship of the *Review* in her absence, an appointment which she often maintained I would be given one day. In recent years she had been training me for such a task and lovingly instilled in me the belief that I could do it.

On many visits to her bedside at the hospital she told me how glad she would be to be released from her body and that her mother, brother and husband were preparing to receive her on the other side of the veil we know as death. She was always of the belief that life did not end with the dying of the body but that the soul travelled on to another life elsewhere.

Interestingly enough, during an earlier session of a two-year course which we both began in 1981 on 'Personal Growth in Human Relations, Pastoral Care & Counselling' run by Dennis Hyde, psychotherapist, we had participated on some group work on dying. During that session I particularly noticed how Clare saw death as a friend and welcomed his arrival. Little did I know at the time that this was the last evening we would attend the course together.

Even while confined to her hospital bed she still felt very restless and longed to return to her work on the magazine. Although in recent years she had wanted so much to retire from her busy life and involvement with the *Review* another part of her found it very difficult to relinquish her commitment to it and truly 'let go'.

On another visit I took a portable cassette player and played her favourite piece of classical music: 'Canon à 3 on a ground in D' by Pachelbel. I well remember the beautiful smile that spread across her peaceful features as she lay so still with her eyes closed listening to its immensely uplifting refrain.

On the morning of 9 March 1983, while alone with her, in the rustle of spring, she quietly left this world.

On her desk by the typewriter I found her last piece of unfinished writing:

THE SPRINGTIME OF THE HEART

It has been a long hard winter for many souls, not only in the world about us, with floods, gale-force winds apart from the continual turmoil which it is said will not abate until the end of the century, but for many individually. Not only have their circumstances brought them problems, but relationships become more difficult as we become more sensitive, more easily irritated, tending to project our own inner disturbances upon those about us. The steadily increasing Light pouring from us on high is, or should be, making us more and more aware, and if we can become sufficiently detached, we give thanks for the increasing self-understanding it brings. But often it is a painful process unless we are prepared to "let go and let God" purify, adjust and transform us so that we may be more worthy vehicles in High service.

During the winter of the heart, we may feel we have come to a dead-end, feel stopped in our tracks, unable to go back or to move forward. Then it is that Nature, the great teacher, can give us more than we can find in any book. Life never stops. The catkin is enfolded in the dying leaf. Directly the roses are no longer with us, the snowdrops appear. The daffodils bloom under and above the snow. The violets appear in sheltered spots, and soon the birds are building their nests, and we lift up our hearts with a new hope.

During the winter of our discontent, there may have been despair, because of deprivations, desires, even the most spiritual never fulfilled, mistakes which we regret, opportunities missed. But the flowers need the nourishing darkness of the earth in which to grow, and so we must give thanks for our own darkness in which the seeds are unfolding, drawn up by the light of the sun ...